HITCHIN ARCADE

Then and Now

Hitchin Arcade

Then and Now

Researched and Written by:

Ellie Clarke
Scilla Douglas
Keith Fitzpatrick-Matthews
Bobbie Harwood
Chris Honey
John Horton
Pauline Humphries
Chris Parker
Carola Scupham
Simon Walker
Brian Worbey

A Hitchin Historical Society Publication

A Hitchin Historical Society Publication 2007
Copyright © Hitchin Historical Society

ISBN 978-0-9552411-2-3

Design, Reprographics and Print by
Digital Imagin, Hitchin, Hertfordshire SG4 0TY (Tel: 01462-442500)

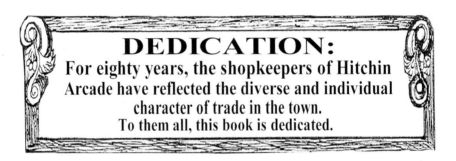

DEDICATION:
For eighty years, the shopkeepers of Hitchin
Arcade have reflected the diverse and individual
character of trade in the town.
To them all, this book is dedicated.

Cover:	Hitchin Arcade from the Market Place 2006 (K. J. Fitzpatrick-Matthews)
Inside Front Cover:	Extract from Ordnance Survey Map 1851 with the Arcade area highlighted (Hitchin Museum)
Half Title Page:	Victorian door latch, 9 The Arcade (drawn by Carola Scupham)
Frontispiece:	Left centre: Swan Commercial Inn and Gatwards Ironmongers next door c.1866 (Hitchin Museum)
Inside Back Cover:	Arcade Roofs 2006 (K. J. Fitzpatrick-Matthews), Night in the Arcade 2005 (Ian Horton)
Back Cover:	The Arcade, looking East, from the car park in 2006 (K. J. Fitzpatrick-Matthews)

ARCADE

Contents

Acknowledgements

The authors would like to thank all those who gave so freely of their time and information in the writing of this book.

Our appreciation is recorded for specialist help provided by Staff at Hertfordshire Archives and Local Studies; by David Hodges, Jenny Oxley and Staff at Hitchin Museum; and by Staff at Hitchin Library. As amateurs, we were fortunate to have the expertise of Archaeology Officer for North Hertfordshire District Council, Keith Fitzpatrick-Matthews.

Valuable assistance was provided by North Hertfordshire District Council, and by Mark Seaman-Hill of Messrs. John Shilcock.

Beryl Church, Claude Geary, Adrian Pomfret and Rodney Wray, Arcade "stalwarts", guided us in the right direction, as did the Gatward and Skeggs families.

Chris Titmus of The Image Studio gave permission to use his "aerial" pohotograph. Ian Horton took dramatic images of the Arcade by night.

Memories bring a book to life. We sincerely thank the following for their recollections and photographs. Sadly, we could not use them all!

Joan Armstrong, Shirley Avery, Marjorie Barrow, Jenny and John Banham, Colin Bates, Cheryl Blundy, Bill Bowker, Mary Bradbeer, Cheryl Catling, Janet Cleverly, Derrick Else, Alan Fleck, Nigel Freeman, Pat Gadd Thurstance, Pat Geary, Janet Hamilton, Bridget Howlett, Jenny Hughes, William Jennings, David Jones, Vic Kirk, Terry Knight, Pamela Lockhart, Pansy Mitchell, Mark Pardoe, Keith Plummer, Hermann Sander, Julie Skinner, Mary Swain, Greta Underwood, Margaret Valentine, Janet Walker, Derek Wheeler, Richard Whitmore, Stuart Wilkins and Judith Wray.

Access to the interiors of Arcade shops was vital. We thank all the retailers for their willing co-operation, which has widened the scope of this book.

The onerous task of proof reading was undertaken by Ann Chambers, Bridget Howlett and Derek Wheeler.

Last, but not least, our sincere thanks to Barrie Dack and his team at Digital Imagin who have once again transformed our disk into a real book!

Any errors or omissions are entirely our own.

Foreword

Hitchin is blest with a wealth of independent retailers. How many towns can still boast a locally owned and run butcher, baker or delicatessen, not to mention fashion, arts, crafts, music shops, cafes and more! This panoply of retailers aims to tempt the shopper away from the main High Street which houses the well-known names of Anytown, U.K. to explore the variety of our historic side streets. Not least amongst these is the Arcade, celebrating its eightieth year and firmly established as a must-see feature of the town and certainly the most picturesque route linking the town centre to the Library, Museum and multi-storey car park.

The history of the Arcade provides a microcosm of trends in retailing since 1927 as illustrated in Appendix 2 and it seems that all the premises were well utilised throughout the period. Indeed the demand for smaller units in Hitchin remains high as people seek to establish themselves in business in a town renowned for its niche retailing.

Over recent years, the Arcade has hosted an Acoustic Stage for Rhythms of the World each July, which has proved extremely popular. New investment in Christmas lights has linked the Arcade to the town scheme and provided a festive welcome to lure the shoppers! And with some co-operative Christmas advertising, the traders work together to proclaim their diversity.

The history of the Arcade is illuminated by the personalities and anecdotes of the past 80 years. The importance of the Arcade to Hitchin today is emphasised by the number of contributors to this book and to those volunteers who undertook the task of collating all the information as a labour of love. Thanks to them all.

The Arcade remains a rich seam of Hitchin's commercial life – long may it remain so.

Keith Hoskins, Hitchin Town Centre Manager
October 2007

Introduction

HOW IT ALL BEGAN

Hitchin people are parochial. We probably have always been parochial and we probably always will be parochial. But we certainly are parochial now, at the beginning of the 21st century!

There is good reason for that, as there is much to be fond of in Hitchin: lovely buildings, varied architecture, interesting nooks and crannies, intriguing alleys and ginnels to draw you through the town as well as fine and unusual shops. None of it is very grand, but most of it is very pleasing and on a relatively small scale. Hitchin town centre was designed for people, and in the 21st century it continues to invite people to wander, explore, shop, relax and enjoy. Nowhere in Hitchin typifies this character more than the Arcade.

Being parochial, we are also protective, and fiercely so at times. It can often help to protect a building or area if it has been well-documented. It became clear to us that the area around the Arcade could be considered "ripe for redevelopment", to use "planning speak". Indeed, as we began working on this project, one area next to the Arcade, which had formerly been small businesses selling and repairing motor vehicles, was already being redeveloped by McCarthy & Stone into accommodation for the more mature generation. A planning application to redevelop Brooker's Yard to housing was under consideration. Suggestions for redeveloping Jackson's Yard, just across West Alley from the Arcade, had been made in the recent past.

Clearly, the area around the Arcade could change considerably in the near future and it was important that the Arcade itself, as well as its setting in the wider townscape, should be protected as much as possible. In early 2005, the question of listing was raised in the local press. In that context, discussions began as to what we could do, and "The Arcade Project" was born.

We didn't know initially what our "Project" was going to be, or who would like to be involved. A bit of publicity through the networks of Hitchin Historical Society and Hitchin Forum produced a group of local residents who either had connections with the Arcade, were interested to learn more about it, or simply had never done this kind of research before and were intrigued. As it happened, these individuals, between them, happily took on researching and documenting the various aspects that appeared to need investigating. Little did we realise that the detective work we would be drawn into, or the intriguing story that would unfold.

Having researched the Arcade, its history, its owners and inhabitants and discovered its particular idiosyncrasies, it seemed perfectly logical to document our findings and share them with the wider Hitchin parochial populace. Now read on ...

Seated round the table (clockwise from front left) Simon Walker, Keith Fitzpatrick-Matthews, John Horton, Carola Scupham, Scilla Douglas, Ellie Clarke, Chris Honey, Chris Parker, Brian Worbey, Pauline Humphries, Bobbie Harwood. November 2006.

The River Hiz at Grove Road: this is how the centre of the town may have looked four thousand years ago, in the Bronze Age

IN THE BEGINNING ...

Prehistory

Hitchin is a place with a long prehistory, stretching back to the time of some of the earliest humans in Britain, the Lower Palaeolithic, around 400,000 years ago. Most of the very early finds come from the eastern side of the town, but distinctive stone tools of the period have also been found in Brand Street, just a short distance north of the Arcade. These early people (who belonged to a different species from ourselves) were attracted to the area because at that time, a large river flowed south through Hitchin towards the precursor of the River Thames and they passed along its banks in search of food and raw materials.

Millennia passed; ice sheets came, went, came back and finally melted about fourteen thousand years ago. Human beings – our ancestors – returned to Britain, bringing a new technology with them: bows and arrows. This invention was essential for hunting in the woodland that now covered much of the landscape. The tools of these people have been found only on the eastern side of the town, and there is environmental evidence that the valley of the River Hiz was marshy at this time, probably forming a braided stream with multiple channels, gradually becoming a periodically flooded water meadow. Where the Arcade now stands would have been on the edge of a swamp, suitable for hunting wildfowl and collecting reeds to make baskets and other useful items.

After about 4300 BC, people (including new settlers from Europe) began to cut down the light woodland that grew on the higher ground to grow crops and keep livestock. Although their tools have been found across Hitchin, none are known from the town centre west of the river; those nearest to the Arcade were found at Wratten Road and suggest domestic activity. It is likely that much of this area was still low-lying and liable to flood.

During the third millennium BC, enormous technological and social changes took place. For the first time, there is evidence of a social elite, its members buried under circular mounds of soil (known as round barrows), accompanied by objects that displayed their wealth and prestige, including items made from the newly discovered material, metal. There are several cemeteries of these mounds in the town, some of them in Priory Park. During excavations at Whitings Court to the south of Arcade Walk, carried out by Pre-Construct Archaeology in 2004, the remains of a levelled burial mound were discovered, but all that survived was the ring-ditch from which the soil to make the mound had been dug. As a result, it is impossible to date the mound more closely than c 2500-1400 BC. The position of the mound, close to the top of the slope, is typical of round barrows, and it is quite possible that it is just one of several forming another cemetery on the slope above what is now Market Place. The excavators have interpreted it as an Iron Age roundhouse, but the width and depth of the ditch are impossibly large and it was clearly the quarry ditch for a central mound.

As the population grew during the second millennium BC, more of the native woodland was cut down to make way for fields, farms and villages. Slowly, the entire landscape was opened up and divided into tribal territories. During the latter part of the millennium, the climate grew much cooler and wetter, making the valley of the River Hiz very unsuitable for habitation again and it is not until the very end of the Iron Age, in the late first century BC, that there is evidence for people living in the centre of Hitchin once more.

The Roman period (AD c 43-450)

It is with these Late Iron Age people that Britain enters recorded history. As is well known, Julius Caesar was north of the Thames in 54 BC and may well have passed close to Hitchin; the Luton archaeologist James Dyer believes that the king he defeated, Cassivellaunus, was based at Ravensburgh, just a few kilometres to the west along the Icknield Way. There would have been little here to interest him, though: most of the evidence we have comes from burials at Burymead, Bancroft and Foxholes, which suggest that there were farms scattered across Hitchin. All of these sites continued to be occupied after the Roman conquest in AD 43 without interruption. Roman pottery, tile and metalwork have been found to the north of the Arcade, in the former cattle market behind The Cock, and immediately to the south, during the 2004 excavations. Little is known about the circumstances of the discoveries in the old cattle market, while those from Whitings Court were not associated with any buildings.

One of the more unusual Roman finds from the town centre was made during the construction of the Corn Exchange in 1853. When the previous building, the seventeenth-century Red Lion public house, was demolished, several fragments of carved marble were found in its foundations. At the time, they were believed to have come from an Etruscan sarcophagus, which could only have arrived in Britain as part of an antiquarian collection; this was thought puzzling, as such collections only began to be made in the eighteenth century, long after the foundations of the Red Lion were laid down. However, a re-examination of the marble in the 1990s showed that the carving more likely dates from the third century AD and is carved in a style popular in the eastern Roman Empire, but also sometimes found in the west. In that case, it could have come from the tomb of a wealthy local Roman, perhaps an owner of the building that was the source of Roman brick and tile found in the tower of St Mary's Church.

By the fourth century, the focus of settlement had shifted to the eastern side of the

The 'Hitchin Marble': part of an apotheosis scene from a third-century sarcophagus found during the building of the Corn Exchange in 1853 (Hitchin Museum)

River Hiz. Finds of third- and fourth-century date have long been reported from Hollow Lane, Queen Street, Garrison Court and St Andrews Place, while excavations at Portmill Lane and St Mary's Square have revealed ditches that may be property boundaries or field boundaries belonging to a village. Part of the cemetery of this community was found in 2002 during excavations at what had been Jeeves Yard and was clearly Christian, with unaccompanied, extended skeletons in graves facing east. Radiocarbon dates from the burials show that the cemetery continued in use from the third to the eighth century. By that time, according to local historians, St Mary's Church had been founded.

ad Hiccum (AD c 650-1300)

It has long been known that the name of the town derives from that of the *Hicce*, a small tribe listed in a seventh-century document, the so-called Tribal Hidage. Curiously, their name derives from a Celtic word meaning 'dry' (*sicca*) rather than an Old English word; there is no need for Reginald Hine's scepticism regarding this derivation. It is likely that they were not invading Saxons but the native people buried in the Queen Street cemetery, who were able to maintain their identity (if not language) during the migration period. By the tenth century, they had a minster church, which medieval tradition said had been founded by King Offa in the 790s.

Numerous place names (including Bearton and Burymead) suggest that Hitchin was classed as a *burh* in the early medieval period. *Burhs* were defended settlements, with a planned street layout, a market and local administrative functions. The plan of modern Hitchin certainly indicates that at least part of it was first laid out on a regular grid, and an analysis by Gil Burleigh and Mark Stevenson suggests that it was a planned town dating from the Late Saxon period, with a defensive bank and ditch running along a line just east of Paynes Park and Coopers Alley. The discovery of a massive V-shaped ditch on exactly this

The probable **burh** *ditch at Paynes Park, excavated in 2004 (© Pre-Construct Archaeology)*

line at Whitings Court in 2004 appears to confirm the suggestion: the size is too large to be a simple property or field boundary; the V-shape is typical of Late Saxon *burh* ditches and it contained some scraps of St Neots type pottery, dating from the ninth to twelfth centuries.

Intriguingly, there were also two short stretches of shallow ditch, one parallel with the back wall of the Arcade, the other parallel with but outside the possible *burh* ditch. They were thought by the excavators to be part of a Roman field system, but the way they follow the medieval boundaries suggests an early medieval origin, perhaps belonging to a town established before the defences were put up.

When might all this have happened? The only way to assess the date is by looking at what else we know about early medieval Hitchin. The medieval tradition that St Mary's was founded in 792 by Offa has no early documentary support, although it has long been accepted by historians. The discovery of clearly ancient foundations beneath the floor of the church in the early twentieth century was also thought to support this date. However, analysis of the recorded foundations shows the earliest phase to have been of basilican form, consisting of a long narrow nave with side aisles, a plan used for regionally important churches during the seventh century. The earlier of the two apses looks like an addition to the original plan, as it is not the same width as the original chancel, and an apse of this type would be more typical of the eighth century. This means that the original foundation of the church almost certainly has to be earlier than Offa and a century or more earlier than the traditional date. If the date 792 has any authority, it might be for the expansion of the chancel into the semicircular apse.

The presence of a regionally important church in seventh-century Hitchin fits in with the mention of the *Hicce* in the Tribal Hidage and shows that the site of the present town was already their main centre. The question that then arises is why such an important

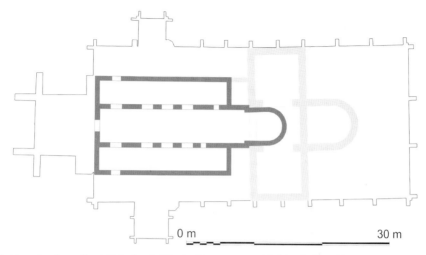

The plan of early medieval St Andrew's Minster (the precursor of St Mary's Church), reconstructed from discoveries in 1911 (K. J. Fitzpatrick-Matthews)

church is not mentioned in any early documents. In a way, this would not be surprising: few documents have survived from early Mercia as a result of the destruction of its government and churches during the ninth- and tenth-century Danish invasions. On the other hand, there is a strong possibility that Hitchin is mentioned frequently, but under a different name. Clifford Offer, a former Rector of Hitchin, has argued persuasively that it was the site of *Clofesho*, the site of numerous synods of the English church between the late seventh century and 825, but a place-name long since lost. Hitchin fits all of the criteria for its location: it is an easily accessible place near London, on the boundary of Mercia and the eighth-century dioceses of Lichfield and London. As with Leeds and Oundle, the modern name of the town derives from the name of the minor kingdom in which it is situated, not the original name of the settlement.

This suggests that the laying out of property boundaries south of the Arcade would be contemporary with the establishment of the church in a newly developing town in the seventh century. Such a town would have been under royal control, in this instance by the sub-king of the Hicce. Offa's reputed interest in Hitchin would be to do with a church established some time before his reign.

By the tenth century, England was a land of developing market towns, some on the sites of Roman towns, others (like Hitchin) newly established in the early Middle Ages. Many continued to be royal possessions, providing revenue, manpower and produce to a typically peripatetic medieval court. Occasionally the royal household might even descend on the place and expect to be fed and watered for the duration. As we have seen, Hitchin seems to have been provided with a defensive bank and ditch around this time. To the west, it followed the line of Paynes Park and Coopers Alley; to the south, it perhaps lay slightly north of Tilehouse Street and Bridge Street, while to the north, it may have been roughly in the position of the nineteenth-century Hermitage Road. Construction of defences on this scale can only have been carried out under royal control.

The church was expanded eastwards, with the addition of transepts and a much larger chancel, creating a church almost as large as the present St Mary's; the plan suggests that it also happened in the tenth century. This would be a plausible date for the creation of a

*The **burh** of Hitchin in the early tenth century (K. J. Fitzpatrick-Matthews)*

burh in the town. This period saw the reconquest of Mercia from the Danes by Æthelflæd (the ruler of Mercia) in the north-west and her brother, Edward the Elder (King of Wessex), in the south-east. Edward's campaigns are poorly documented, although it is known that he established two *burhs* at Hertford. Hitchin (together with Bedford and, probably, Ashwell) would have been fortified as part of his campaigns along the eastern border of Mercia.

We do not know why the defences of Hitchin did not survive into the High Middle Ages; they were so thoroughly obliterated that no-one even suspected that they might have existed until the 1990s. At Hertford, the ditch of the southern *burh* had been filled in by the early eleventh century and it is likely that the same happened at Hitchin, as indicated by the lack of finds in its deliberate backfill. The military situation of the early tenth century that had led to their construction was long in the past and no longer applied: new solutions to the Viking threat were being worked out (including a national tax and electing one of their leaders – Cnut – to be king of England). The town was not considered of strategic importance at the time of the Norman Conquest or the Civil War during the reigns of Stephen and Matilda, so a castle was not built here; instead, they were established at either end of the Hitchin Gap (at Great Wymondley, Pirton and Cainhoe), protecting the town from the outside. It is curious that no burgesses were recorded for the town in Domesday Book (although fourteen were recorded at Ashwell), but it is possible that this is an error of omission (it does not mention a priest, for instance, even though the Minster is named) and it was certainly recorded as a borough in 1268. It is also possible that it ceased to be classed as a *burh* when the defences were razed. Its status as a royal manor at the time of the conquest, when it was the largest royal demesne in the county, was presumably inherited from its status as the *caput* (head place) of the *regio* (minor kingdom) of the Hicce. Tovi Pruda's donation of the estate to his foundation at Waltham Abbey, its alienation to the crown under his son Athelstan, its subsequent rededication to the Abbey by the king in Earl Harold's charter of 1062 and the possession of the manor by the crown in 1086 probably reflects the complex politics of the first half of the eleventh century.

There is little reason to suspect that the Market Place was created after the Norman Conquest, as Gil Burleigh and Mark Stevenson thought, as it appears to be an integral element in the layout of property boundaries, as shown by the plan of the *burh* on page 6 Indeed, its form is typical of the broad market street found in many Mercian towns whose origins go back to the Middle Saxon period, c 650-850. It is noticeable how its apex appears to be slightly north of the junction between Bancroft and Hermitage Road, at the point where a change in the alignment of property boundaries suggests that they were laid out where the northern line of the defences can be conjectured to have lain but at a later date.

The High Medieval town is little known archaeologically. The most significant surviving monument is the parish church, all of which, in its present form, is later than the hurricane of 1115, which seems to have destroyed the old Minster, if it had not already been rebuilt in the eleventh century. Pottery kilns have been found east of Bancroft and at the western end of Tilehouse Street (in the latter case, two separate dumps of spoiled pots – wasters – rather than the actual kiln were found). These can be dated to the thirteenth century and their location within a town is unusual, as they were more conveniently situated close to sources of fuel.

During the excavation to the south of the Arcade in 2004, a number of twelfth to fourteenth century pits were found. This is typical of medieval urban properties. Although they are often identified as 'rubbish pits', they rarely contain much in the way of rubbish and their function is not often clear. One curious feature was cut into the edge of the backfilled *burh* ditch. Consisting of a circular pit with a short gully running into it, the base was lined with rammed chalk with a concave surface, which had traces of burning at its centre. It seems to have been industrial in some way, and although the temperatures reached were not high enough for it to have been a kiln and its function remains unknown at present, it was evidently used to heat something.

There were also traces of buildings, represented by postholes, but they were too scattered and disturbed by later activity to make meaningful patterns by which buildings could be identified. Buildings in this position could have been additional accommodation, counting houses, warehouses, sheds or any one of a variety of low-status urban structures. The western edge of the property was marked by a ditch that lay further west than the *burh* ditch and close to the line of the possible seventh-century ditch. There is little doubt that the archaeology of Arcade Walk and the car park would be almost identical.

The later Middle Ages (c 1300-1550)

If archaeological evidence for the High Medieval town is sparse, that for the Late Middle Ages is almost non-existent, apart from a rich legacy of standing buildings. It has been proposed that Old Park Road takes its name from a deer park established during this period, while the ponds that lent their name to Fishponds Road, at the northern limit of the town, were probably also dug around this time. The 2004 excavation south of the Arcade produced less evidence from this period than the preceding, apart from a few pits and postholes. The excavator has suggested that the site reverted to agricultural or horticultural land during the fifteenth century. This would fit with the likely drop in population following the disasters of the fourteenth century (the famines of the early decades and the Black Death of the middle decades). Nevertheless, the town clearly remained prosperous, with most of the surviving work in the parish church dating from this time. It is possible that the soil at Whitings Court is evidence for this prosperity: rather than being productive horticultural or agricultural land, it is just as likely to have belonged to a formal garden.

By the end of the period, at the time of the Dissolution, *The Swane Inn* had been established at the eastern end of the site and, as will be seen in the next chapter, parts of it survive unexpectedly encapsulated in the nineteenth-century properties at the front of the Arcade. Owned by The Brotherhood, a religious fraternity established as the Guild of Our Lady in 1475, it was first recorded in 1539, nine years before the suppression of the guild and the seizure of its properties. It is possible that some of the unknown buried archaeology of the site would give an insight into when the guild acquired the property and what use they made of it. Whether there is any connection between the guild and the suspected original name of West Alley – Corpus Christi Alley – is not known. With the close of the Middle Ages and the dismantling of its religious institutions, we enter the era of recorded history.

No part of the Arcade, Arcade Walk or the car park to the west has ever been excavated. The large excavation of 2004 at Whitings Court, to the south, is the only controlled archaeological work to have taken place close by. The former Field Archaeology Section of North Hertfordshire District Council hand-excavated a number of tree-planting holes in Market Place in November and December 1993, when they discovered at least eight earlier surfaces reaching back to the later medieval period. Other than this, we have

Brotherhood Hall, Bancroft: home of the guild that owned The Swan; there were originally ridge tiles at either end of the roof with horseman figurines on top (as seen in the next illustration)

to rely on conjecture. Today, archaeological excavation is most commonly carried out in advance of development, thanks to current planning legislation and guidance, usually where there is going to be disturbance of the ground.

The rare horseman ridge tile from the Brotherhood Hall, now in Hitchin Museum (Drawing probably by William Dawson)

Chapter 2

"AT THE SIGN OF THE SWANE"

Let us travel back in time nearly 500 years, to the reign of Henry VIII, and stand in Hitchin's Market Place. In front of us, looking towards the west, on the spot now occupied by our present Arcade and O2, we would have seen a thriving Tudor inn, set in the muddy bustle of a small market town. It would be there both to satisfy the needs of travellers for food, drink, a bed and fresh horses or stabling, and to support the local community with warmth, companionship, entertainment and a place in which to transact business.

The first recorded reference to "the Swane" occurs in 1539. It was the property of a religious guild called The Brotherhood, and it was let to George Kente for 40 years at an annual rent of £3.6.8d (£3.33), which amount included the use of twelve and a half acres of land. Nine years later the ownership of the property had changed, but "Mine Host" was still in occupation. The Brotherhood was The Guild of Our Lady established in 1475, during the reign of Edward IV. A group of rich Hitchin wool merchants was licensed by the king to found the fraternity, which was granted valuable financial rights in the town, providing support for two chaplains to say prayers for the brotherhood and sisters of the fraternity. A surviving list enumerates, amongst other properties and benefits, the Inn, the Brotherhood House in Bancroft, and five stallages in Market Place. The Guild was suppressed and its properties seized by the king in 1548. The Swane and other properties were sold to Ralph (or Ranulph) Burgh and Robert Beverly. About this time, documents show that the Inn's name becomes formalised, with the 'e' disappearing.

Life was about to become difficult for the landlord. In 1552 Justices of the Peace were given the new duty of licensing inns, taverns and alehouses. In the "good old days" a landlord could rule his own house, set his closing hours (if any), and allow any pastime he saw fit to take place. The era of progressive regulation had dawned: the "convenient lodgings and good and wholesome victuals" were only beginning. Now he was responsible for the conduct of those he lodged ... and dice, cards, tennis, bowls were (supposedly) out!

Currently we can only speculate on the appearance of the early inn, but intriguing clues, unearthed during the writing of this book, suggest that important elements of the timber-framed structure may well survive both inside the shell of today's No.1 The Arcade and No.33 Market Place. Moulding along the edges of ancient timbers suggests a high-status building, probably the remains of the 16th century Swan Inn. The room above the entrance to the modern Arcade would have been a chamber above the entrance to the Swan's courtyard, possibly occupied by the landlord or wealthier guests.

"Murder most foul".

Move on 60 years or so: we next discover that on 17th July 1618, *"at the Swan in Hitchin, belonging to Edward Jeve"* a local barber Edward Troyton (or Troughton) was being indicted for *"felonious killing"*.

Three days earlier, at the inn, Troyton and Richard Tristram, a yeoman, had quarrelled over a game of dice. Tristram *"snatched up the stakes"* from the table, Troyton drew his

sword, and ran him through the chest. He died two days later. The crime is listed in the Hertfordshire Indictments (Calendar of Assize Records, James I). The verdict was *"guilty to hang"* although a stay of execution was granted until 1st September. Interestingly the Coroner is a John *Jeve* and the jury is headed by an Adam *Tristram*.

Historically, things go quiet after this. In 1656 a John Hurst "at the sign of the Swan in Hitchin" is licensed to keep a tavern and *"sell Wyne by retail"*. In an era when running water formed a convenient sewer and rubbish tip, beer was a universal beverage, wine an addition for the upper classes. Beer was an anaesthetic, it was safe and sustaining, and no doubt it

A Game of Dice
(History of Hitchin R.L. Hine)

blurred susceptibilities to conditions that were by our standards, cold, hard and squalid. At this time most inns would have brewed their own beer, and we have no reason to think that the Swan did otherwise.

The Great Outdoors

Records give us an indication of conditions outside the Inn. In 1697, a *"Richard Rayner, gent,"* was reported for failing to keep in repair the causeway leading *"unto the Gutter which runneth from the sign of the Swan to the sign of the Angell"* (in Sun Street). We also learn of the presence of Butchers' stalls in the Shambles. These were two parallel rows of buildings that stood in Market Place fronting the site of what is now the Corn Exchange (they can be seen clearly on old maps of the town – see inside front cover, the last being demolished in 1856). Conditions at the Swan gateway must have been far from ideal. Carts and wheeled-vehicles were not common on English roads until the 17th century, most goods being carried by packhorses. Drovers from the Highlands brought their cattle through the town on the way to London, and it became a regular stopping place. The produce of the Hitchin area, grain and wool, would have been sold to buy items not available locally. All this activity would have generated business for a Swan landlord, as it would have done for other inns in the town. Moving on fifty years, to when the Hitchin to Bedford Turnpike Trust sought to get a grip on the chaos, we read that the Trustees bought and removed a stall standing on the north side of the Inn gateway. This enabled the road into Market Place to be widened, and would doubtless make the sweep into the yard less hazardous.

By the middle of the 18th century the turnpike trusts had made a huge impact on road conditions, and, from the early nineteenth century, new surfaces pioneered by Telford and McAdam improved things further. These changes were seen locally when the Welwyn Trust was set up in 1726, and following a petition, it extended its range in 1738, north of Stevenage, from Corey's Mill to Hitchin. In 1763 it took over the route between Welwyn and Hitchin via Codicote. In 1757 the Bedford to Hitchin turnpike opened with a tollgate in Ickleford. So by the beginning of the 19th century local roads, indeed English roads, had improved enormously and journeys of all types in a variety of vehicles were achieving speeds never before imagined: stagecoaches, mail coaches, private gigs, carts. A travel manual in the possession of the writer dating from this time shows the map of England traversed by a 'spider's web' of roads, with full details of routes, distances and principal sights.

Entertaining the military

One of the less profitable obligations of the poor licensee was that of billeting troops and horses, on the march or in quarters. Army barracks did not exist until the 19th century, and the low rates paid to the innkeeper in compensation plus the rule that, if need be, other occupants could be turned out (even family members) made this legal duty highly unpopular. In the Civil War, Hitchin was home to 3,000 Parliamentary troops, so no doubt the Swan Inn suffered in this way. Overseers' Records for 1732 show a payment of 1/8d (8p) for "*Soldiers at the Swan*", and we find a bill from Richard Atkin, a butcher in Bucklersbury, for meat for the Volunteers in 1802.

Hosting troops might have been a downside of "Swan" life, but in other respects business was expanding. Increased trade would have brought increased prosperity and this would have been reflected in changes and developments to the structures of both the inn and its yard. The brief survey of the buildings, both fronting and in the present Arcade area itself, chart the story of a business which responded to demand and the opportunity to invest. It appears that the inn yard underwent considerable extension during the late 18th century, and roof structures and brickwork indicate expansion over a variety of periods. At some time before photography was available to record the Swan facade, the whole frontage was fashionably refaced in brick, hiding its timber framework.

The Kershaw dynasty

Certain trades and professions tend to run in families and at the "Swan" we see an example of two running side by side, one no doubt supporting the other: coaching and innkeeping.

Jonas Kershaw, proprietor of the Hitchin stagecoach that made journeys to London several times a week, was landlord until 1805. We know both from Licencing and

Ratepayers' Records that George Kershaw was proprietor of The Swan Inn from 1806 until 1824, and The Hertfordshire Express of 1850 reminds us that Kershaw's Coach was "owned and horsed by members of the same family for 109 consecutive years." An advertisement of 1808 informs us that:

1808 Advertisement for the Post Coach (Hitchin Museum)

.HITCHIN,

STEVENAGE, WELLWYN, & HATFIELD,

Post Coach,

SETS out from the SWAN INN, Hitchin, every Monday, Wednesday, and Friday Morning, precisely at Eight o'Clock,—and arrives at the Greyhound, West Smithfield at Half past One,—returns from thence every Tuesday, Thursday, and Saturday Morning at the same Hour, and arrives at Hitchin at Two.

Performed by

G. & R. KERSHAW.

Who return their sincere Thanks to their Friends for all Favors received, and beg leave to inform them, that they will endeavour, by the strictest Attention in every Department, to merit a continuance of the same.

Time of leaving each Place in the Morning.

Swan, ... *Hitchin,* . . . . at Eight o'Clock.
White Lion, ... *Stevenage,* . . . . Half past Eight.
Roe Buck, ... *Broadwater,* . . . . . Quar. bef. Nine.
Rose & Crown, . . *Wellwyn,* . . . . Half past Nine.
Bell, ... *Hatfield,* . . . . Half past Ten.

Where Places may be taken by applying early the Day before.

N. B. The Proprietors will not be accountable for Parcels above Five Pounds Value, except entered, and paid for accordingly.

J. Bedford, Printer, Hitchin.

(Incidentally, George Kershaw built "Charnwood", now Hitchin Museum, in 1825, just before his death in 1826)

John Kershaw appeared on the voter's list as *"Swan innkeeper"* in 1836, and again on the Ratepayers list in 1838 *(house, brewhouse, yard, stables and garden £42.0.0)*. The Hertfordshire Express of August 1850 reported that he made journeys to London on the Coachman's Box for nearly 40 years, and according to Reginald Hine was reputed to be such an accomplished whip that *"he could take a fly off a leader's ear"*. But more of the Kershaw connection later.

Business as usual

As the nineteenth century progressed it becomes easier to discover how the "Swan" fitted into the local scene. Each decade brought increasing national and local bureaucracy. From 1841 onwards we have the Census, and more lists of all types, backed up by a serious and reliable local press, which thrived on detail.

The 1841 census (not wholly accurate) gives us John Fleck<u>more</u> (aged 26) innkeeper, his wife Marianne (27) and two small children in residence at the Swan. (By 1845, it was generally referred to as "The Swan Commercial Inn".) In 1846, he was still innkeeper but Harriet Lewin was noted as owner (more of her later).

The 1851 Census is a more workmanlike affair. John Fleck<u>noe</u> (note the correction of the surname) was still "Mine Host" and wife Mary A. (*sic*) had been busy producing another four children, as well as supervising a band of young live-in staff: a barmaid, two general servants and a waiter. We know that the arrival of the railway in Hitchin in August 1850 put an almost instantaneous end to the coach trade, the Kershaw family themselves being swift to auction off their livestock and vehicles. It is no surprise to read in a Directory of 1853 that the Swan sent an *"omnibus to meet every train"*, adaptability to circumstances being essential business practice.

There was obviously a short interregnum in 1853 as the Flecknoes disappeared from the scene. That year was also the time of the horrific Gatward fire (of which more later), which was reported in the Hertfordshire Express of 26th March.

In 1853 John Gatward was operating a successful business at No.2 High Street, separated from the "Swan" at street frontage by a little shop kept by Samuel Prudden. Gatward also ran a small iron foundry, situated behind his shop, adjacent to the inn yard. A glance at the 1878 Sale Plan (see page 18) will alert you to the density of buildings on the site and the potential risks this entailed. When disaster struck one March night in 1853, acting "Swan" landlord, George Lewin, with another neighbour, alerted by noise from the street, *"arrived on the spot, and with great promptitude, proceeded to the back entrance of the house … these gentlemen immediately forced the door and proceeding upstairs to the sleeping apartments of Mr and Mrs Gatward, aroused them."*

When the Hitchin fire engines arrived on the scene, it was found that the Gatward premises were beyond saving. *"… the attention of the firemen was, therefore, directed to the adjoining premises, which were now on fire. The house of Mr Samuel Prudden, ironmonger, adjoining the Swan Inn, the dining room and billiard room of the Swan Inn, which adjoined the back part of Mr Gatward's premises … were in danger of falling prey to the devouring element; and the most energetic, but not entirely successful, efforts were made to save them … The damage done by the fire is very considerable … The shop and house of Mr Prudden, ironmonger, are also destroyed and the roof and floor of the "Swan" billiard room which extended over Mr Prudden's house … All these gentlemen are insured, but whether to the full value of their losses we are not informed."*

Local assumption has always been that the Gatward fire caused irreparable damage to the fabric of the "Swan" resulting in the obliteration of its historic features and the need for substantial demolition and rebuilding work. Although the fire was a disaster in human terms, structural damage appears to have been more limited.

This supposition is now even more open to re-interpretation, following our building investigations of 2006. Large portions of the old inn's timber framework remain in the upper storeys of the buildings fronting the present Arcade, and upstairs in the present bookshop premises, teasing the experts to uncover more. No doubt fire damage was sustained during the episode; indeed a look at the roof trusses in the north range of buildings in Arcade Walk (stables and corn lofts in 1853), show that this roof at least had to be replaced.

In 1854 we learn that the Inn was being run by "S. Prudden and others", with Harriet Lewin the owner. Was this the Mr. Samuel Prudden next door, rendered homeless by events?

Things settled down again in 1855 when Richard Wadlow became publican, moving from a job as beer retailer in Walsworth Road. The 1861 census tells us that he was a widower aged 43, born in Benington, and his household included three young sons, his niece as housekeeper, and his brother John, described as a groom. In addition there were "live in" staff: a cook, a waitress and a "boots" James Cooper (aged 21) born in Hitchin. Census night also records three visitors.

Travellers came and went, but the "locals" were there forever, and a wise landlord was careful to foster links within the town. Traditionally, inns played a pivotal role in community life. They served as places of business, informal seats of local government, convenient meeting places for local organisations, and very importantly, as places of entertainment.

'Supper at the Swan.' From a sketch by Samuel Lucas 1845. (Hitchin Museum)

Looking through contemporary newspapers we find that the Swan filled all these roles. A visit to the museum archive was also useful. An early receipted bill (1816) is reproduced below.

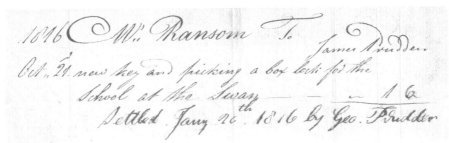

Mr Ransom's receipt. It reads: "Oct.21st 1816. Mr Ransom To James Prudden new key and picking a box lock for the School at the Swan 1s 6d. Settled January 26th 1816 by Geo. Prudden." (Hitchin Museum) Note the inconsistency in the dates! 1s 6d is the equivalent of 7 ½ p today.

(Amazing how these Pruddens keep popping up!)

The Ransom family were Quaker businessmen and philanthropists who were probably involved in running an Adult School in a room at the Inn.

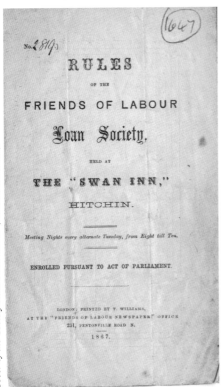

Cover of the Society Rule Book 1867. (Hitchin Museum)

The newspaper archive tells us that the "Swan" hosted a Public Dinner in July 1832 to celebrate the passing of the new Parliamentary Reform Act. In June 1835 we read that it was the meeting place of the local Board of Guardians, who administered the Union Workhouse at Chalkdell, giving *"Justice to the poor, integrity to the Ratepayer"* as one local member promised. That meeting appointed two Relieving Officers. "The Friends of Labour Loans Association" met at the Inn. The Museum holds a Society Rule Book dated 1867.

It existed to assist members with small loans, repayable by instalments. In effect, it was an early Benefit Society, offering: *"Meeting Nights every alternate Tuesday, from Eight till Ten"*.

Together with several other local hostelries, the Inn was traditionally the home of entertainment. The Swan had a stage and regularly put on plays, often blood-curdling melodramas, at tuppence a head. In August 1865, The Hertfordshire Express advertised the *"Exhibition of the Extraordinary Blue and Flesh Coloured HAIRLESS HORSE from the South of Africa"* to take place at the Swan. One wonders if the poor beast made a stage appearance, or if he took up residence in the yard? As a freak show this rated as relatively tasteful.

Blood is thicker than water...?

There is a precise date for the arrival of the final landlord. On 18th January 1868, the Hertfordshire Express carried an advertisement.

William Lewin came from a well-known local inn-keeping family. Lewins were over the

---

SWAN COMMERCIAL HOTEL,
MARKET SQUARE, HITCHIN.

WILLIAM LEWIN

BEGS to announce that he has taken the above Hotel, and respectfully solicits a continuance of the support which has been afforded his predecessor.

Wines and Spirits of the finest quality kept in stock.

Swan Commercial Inn advertisement 1868. (Hitchin Museum)

road at The George until its closure in 1870. But William's personal circumstances made his arrival at The Swan almost a matter of course. His obituary in the North Hertfordshire and South Bedfordshire Journal, dated March 1904, gives an illuminating picture of his life and character.

William's father had been a publican at the Red Lion in Market Place, before it made way for the Corn Exchange and moved to Bucklersbury, a trade that he dovetailed with that of butcher. He died early, in 1843 (William Lucas' Diary cites drink as the cause), and Harriet Lewin, widow, was left to run the Inn. This Harriet Lewin was *"a daughter of the late Mr. Kershaw, driver of the Hitchin Coach"*, according to the 1904 obituary.

Our William Lewin was his eldest son, working as a carpenter in London at the time of his father's death. *"He was his mother's favourite and she longed for his return home. He obliged her, came back to Hitchin and went into business with his brother as a butcher. Things did not go smoothly, the partnership was dissolved and William then commenced a brewing business in Portmill Lane. In 1864 this moved to premises at the Triangle but large brewers 'squeezed him and other small ones out'."* Fortunately, by now, his mother Harriet Lewin was owner of the Swan, and William and his young family took over the tenancy.

On the 1871 Census we find him (aged 52) with his wife Emma (35) and two little daughters, Harriet Kershaw Lewin (4) and a new baby. Living-in staff included a waitress, a cook, two nursemaids and a "boots." William was also licensed to let horses and flys (light, two-wheeled, one horse carriages) between 1870 and 1882, and joined with The Sun Inn in a triangular commuter run to and from the railway station.

On Tuesday 16th July 1878, auctioneer George Jackson sold the freehold of The Swan

Hotel, "*stabling, lofts, and large yard, together with various adjacent plots of garden ground*".
The valuable Lewin (Kershaw) estate was being dismantled following Harriet Lewin's
death. George Lewin (a family member) bought the Inn, stabling, lofts and yard for £2,700
plus £105 for fixtures. The whole family estate realised a total of over £7,000. Neighbour
John Gatward shrewdly purchased five plots, putting in place a strategy that bore fruit a few
years later.

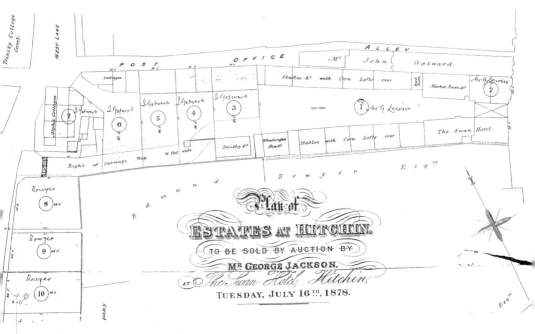

Swan Yard & Hotel Estates Plan and Sale Document 1878. (Hitchin Museum)

William Lewin may have continued as licensee under the new management for a short
period. A billboard for the inn in 1881 mentioned that he was also a wine and spirit
merchant. One wonders if he was aware of the fate that was about to befall him?

In 1884 George Lewin, unable to resist temptation, sold The Swan and the yard to John
Gatward for £3,715, thus making a very handsome profit over six years.

Public sympathy was obviously roused on behalf of William and his family. Just before
Christmas that same year, The Hertfordshire Express announced the setting-up of The
William Lewin Fund to help him in "*the unfortunate circumstances in which he finds himself,
owing to the sale of the house and its diversion to other uses, without any compensation for the
loss of goodwill*". Blood was obviously not thicker than water at the end of the day. William
Lewin at 65 years of age was out of a job.

However, William lived on to enjoy an active old age, until aged 85, *"frail and with failing eyesight"* he was knocked down by a baker's cart in the High Street, and died at home of a fractured skull.

The newspaper obituary of 1904 paints a touching portrait of William Lewin both as a landlord and as a man.

"He gained for himself a name of high repute among the commercial and travelling public for the admirable catering always to be found at The Swan. He conducted his house with the greatest of order, in the opinion of some a little too much so, and during the whole of his tenancy no word was ever raised against it by the police or the public."

"Although brought down in circumstances through no fault of his own, he always exhibited that gentlemanly and intelligent behaviour for which he was previously well known."

He is buried in Hitchin cemetery.

The Swan yard

A coaching inn would only have been as successful as its yard. Careful scrutiny of the 1878 Estates Plan and Sale Document helps us to appreciate what a large and convenient addition this must have been to The Swan. The yard had stabling and lofts on both sides plus wheelwrights and a smithy. In addition to other large side-buildings used as workshops, it had the added benefit of a Right of Carriageway, 16 feet wide, into West Lane (Paynes Park). Although "lane" would have probably described its condition in earlier times, this handy exit from the premises must have helped ease "bottlenecks" at the Market Place entrance. There were also a total of eight small cottages at the top of the yard with Census evidence that some occupiers were Swan employees.

A coaching yard was a vibrant place, full of bustle, noise and acrid smells. Horses, carts and carriages would have clattered under the arch, all working to a tight schedule, with a need for bait, rest and running repairs. Yard work was highly skilled and a combination of trades seemed to have worked in close proximity. The 1841 census shows us Joseph Stevens (Ostler, Swan Inn) at one of the yard cottages. In 1851 his wife is shown as a cook and by 1861 their son William is a "Swan" groom. The services of farriers (blacksmiths), harness makers and saddlers would also have been needed. A yard was a "one stop shop" where skilled craftsmen were alert to emergencies and had the materials and expertise to keep horses and vehicles on the road. William Lewin's resident *"horses and flys"* would also have been beneficiaries of these services.

But it was not all equine pampering. In the Museum there is an advertisement dated August 1872 (see over) promoting the Coach Building and Wheelwright business of Alfred Rogers. He may well have occupied the premises identified on the 1878 sale plan, conveniently next to the Smithy.

William Beaver, a basket maker, and brother of well-known surveyor George and postmaster John, had a workshop in the yard. Uriah Holloway, a cooper (barrel maker) also occupied yard premises.

A. ROGERS,
COACHBUILDER AND WHEELWRIGHT,

RETURNS his sincere thanks for the support he has received since his commencement in Business, and begs most respectfully to inform his patrons and the Gentry and Public generally of Hitchin and the neighbourhood that he has taken the Premises in the

SWAN INN YARD, HITCHIN,

Lately occupied by Mr. HERBERT WINCH, where he intends carrying on the COACH BUILDING Business in all its Branches, in addition to the Business which he carries on at the King's Arms Inn Yard, Bucklersbury, Hitchin.

REPAIRS punctually and carefully attended to.

Alfred Rogers advertisement 1872. (Hitchin Museum)

Just to the right of the coaching arch were two important offices vital to the smooth running of a market town. The Market Room (site of the present Book Bug) presumably filled a role similar to that of the present day Market Offices: taking rents and bookings and sorting out problems. Remember that the market itself was situated only a few yards away. Next-door was a small "Bank Room".

By the 1880s the Hitchin branch of the Wells, Hogge and Lindsell Bank had a small office in the Swan Yard. It was originally only open on Tuesdays (Market Day) but grew so busy that it later provided a daily service. Over time it became the Capital and Counties Bank Ltd and was still trading in the town in 1900.

So William Lewin would not have been the only local businessman to recoil in shock in 1884, when George Lewin capitalised on his "Swan" investment. But offices could find alternative premises. The sale to John Gatward resulted in the break-up of a little interdependent craft community with roots stretching back over three hundred years, skills which had been nurtured and practised right in the heart of Hitchin, *"at the sign of the Swane"*.

The sign of the Swan, from an engraving by the Bedford architect John Sunman Austin. The name "Flecknoe" is visible. According to the census, John Flecknoe was 26 years old in 1841. He was still there in 1851, but in 1853 had disappeared.

Market Place with Swan Iron Works sign in foreground 1893. (Hitchin Museum)

Chapter 3

THE GATWARD CONNECTION

If a stranger to Hitchin asked you where Gatward's shop was you would assume they meant the jeweller's in Market Place, but 80 to 170 years earlier you might have enquired whether they wanted the ironmongers instead. This occupied the building that frames the Arcade entrance in Market Place, a development of the old Swan Inn, which John Gatward junior purchased in 1884. Previously the business of John Gatward and Son had been in a prominent position next door, beside the inn yard entrance in Cock Street, later named High Street.

An entry in the 1850 Post Office Directory described it as *"General and Furnishing ironmongers, kitchen range and stove manufacturers, gas, hot water and steam fitters, engineers, iron and brass founders and agricultural implement makers"*.

We need to go further back in time to find out about the connection between the two trades. It was John Gatward senior who branched out into the ironmongery business in Cock Street around 1835, whilst still retaining premises as a watchmaker in Sun Street. He had inherited the firm from his father Benjamin, who in turn had received it from James Gatward who started clock and watch making in 1760. The 'heavy' and 'light' engineering activities were separated by John's sons; Willson Gatward ran the

This Victorian oven door (part of a kitchen range) can be seen in Hitchin Museum

watch making and jewellery trade, now moved to Market Place, leaving the ironmongery to John junior. The former survives to this day, but the latter having been hugely successful in

Victorian times faltered after the First World War and finally closed in 1929. Read more about this later.

John Gatward junior greatly developed and expanded the ironmongery and foundry firm, heading it for possibly forty years. The engineering business also included tin, copper and

The Gatward Business Dynasty

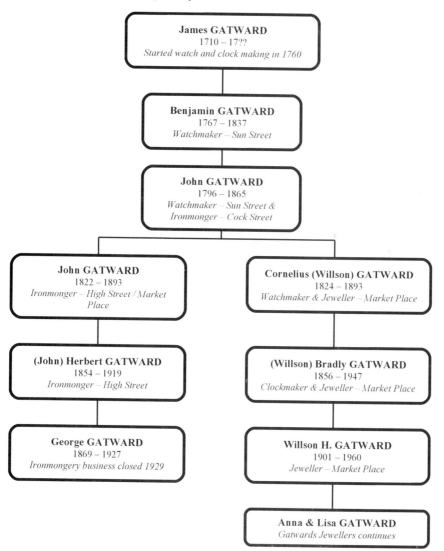

James GATWARD
1710 – 17??
Started watch and clock making in 1760

Benjamin GATWARD
1767 – 1837
Watchmaker – Sun Street

John GATWARD
1796 – 1865
Watchmaker – Sun Street &
Ironmonger – Cock Street

John GATWARD
1822 – 1893
Ironmonger – High Street / Market Place

Cornelius (Willson) GATWARD
1824 – 1893
Watchmaker & Jeweller – Market Place

(John) Herbert GATWARD
1854 – 1919
Ironmonger – High Street

(Willson) Bradly GATWARD
1856 – 1947
Clockmaker & Jeweller – Market Place

George GATWARD
1869 – 1927
Ironmongery business closed 1929

Willson H. GATWARD
1901 – 1960
Jeweller – Market Place

Anna & Lisa GATWARD
Gatwards Jewellers continues

zinc plate workers, braziers, whitesmiths and locksmiths as well as bell hangers. In 1860 George Prudden's gas fitting business was purchased with all its stock, and Gatward was appointed fitter to the burgeoning Hitchin Gas Company founded some thirty years earlier.

Undoubtedly there were some difficult times for the business. One most notably was the tragedy in 1853, when fire broke out *"at Gatward's furnishing and ironmongery warehouse in High Street"* as vividly reported in the Hertfordshire Express. At about a quarter past eleven on Tuesday 26 March some passers by observed smoke issuing from the crevices of the door and shutters of the shop and immediately gave the alarm. Attempts to rouse the Gatwards, who were reposing in the rear of the property, finally succeeded when the back door in Post Office Alley was forced by neighbours. They had time to dress, and John was proceeding downstairs with a box of valuable documents when he was suddenly overpowered by a dense volume of smoke. *"As soon as he partially recovered he called out "Wife come down". There was no answer to this appeal"* and he was then *"beaten back by the smoke and flames"*. It was supposed that Mrs Gatward had proceeded to the front apartment to secure some valuables, since early on Wednesday morning her remains were discovered in the cellar there. *"The house was completely gutted and a greater part of his stock in trade is destroyed, also the house and shop of Mr Prudden"*, adjoining the Swan, *"and roof and floor of the Swan billiard room"*.

JOHN GATWARD, J^{nr} *died*
IRONMONGER. *1893*
1. *purchased The Old Swan Hotel*
in 1864 for £3715.

John Gatward Junior (1822-1893) (Hitchin Museum)

This was joined to the back part of Mr Gatward's premises. The Hertfordshire Mercury added that *"several explosions of gunpowder were heard during the fire but the quantities must have been small or greater damage would have occasioned. 130 lbs of gunpowder at the back of the premises was fortunately removed before the fire reached it."* However, the extent of the damage was mainly due to the delay caused by firemen having to lay water pipes all the way from the Priory horse pond. Also when the Hitchin engines arrived, *"the premises of Mr Gatward were so much in the power of the flames that it was hopeless to save them"*.

However, twenty years later the company seems to be in robust health. An extract from the Hertfordshire News about the Hertfordshire Agricultural Society Show held on the meadows known as Fishpond Closes in Hitchin, amongst other observations, reports on the agricultural implements. *"Messrs Perkins and Gatward were the chief and indeed nearly the only exhibitors. The machines and implements shown by them must have exceeded £4,000 in value."* Corn dressing and blowing machines, cattle and sheep cribs, stackers and elevators, reaping and mowing machines, ploughs and rollers and sowing drills were displayed and demonstrated.

John next comes to prominence in a newspaper report of 1878 about an auction, on 16

July, of the "*Swan Hotel situate in the Market Square Hitchin*". 'The second lot consisted of the house and shop adjoining and forming part of Mr Gatward's ironmongery stores'. It was sold to Mr George Lewin, who also purchased "*the hotel with the stabling, lofts and large yard*". Gatward himself bought "*the upper part of what has hitherto been known as the Swan Yard, with large side buildings used as shops*" and two lots in the "*garden ground running towards Tilehouse Street*". Just six years later, in 1884, John purchased the hotel for £3,715.

By 1870 Gatward had not only reoccupied No 2 High Street but also spread into No 1 (Hitchin Museum)

Thus the ironmongery store occupied the converted hotel building (notice the difference in the façade), and to the rear he added a glazed roof (it, or a replacement, still covers the Arcade) enabling the enclosed area to be used as a furniture showroom. He sold "*good and cheap suites of furniture for sitting rooms and bedrooms, bedsteads and bedding, mail carts and perambulators, easy chairs etc*".

Evidence of this conversion in the form of two cast iron columns, one bearing Gatward's name, can be found in the premises recently occupied by Pomfret's shoe shop. The iron works were situated in the Swan Yard behind the store, with the foundry beside West Alley.

According to the Hertfordshire Mercury (24 June, 1893), both Johns, father and son, were well respected; their "*character for integrity and capacity stood very high*". Both worked all their lives,

The new shop after 1884 (pictured in 1895) with its large, cast iron framed, display windows. You can see the workshops and cottages through the archway (Hitchin Museum)

The shop interior with furniture and furnishings in fashion at the time (from The Official Programme of the Hitchin Celebration of the Coronation of the King. Paternoster & Hales 1902)

John senior in his seventieth year being taken ill six weeks before dying *"at his residence in the Churchyard"*, in August 1865, after a fishing expedition. The shops closed in Hitchin when his procession passed. John junior died aged seventy in June 1893 *"after a fit of apoplexy and paralysis"* just a week earlier. Evidence of his trading success can be deduced from his will; he bequeathed nearly £14,000, over six times the amount left by his watch-making brother Cornelius, who died in the same year.

John junior's son Herbert Gatward married his cousin, Alice, the daughter of George Jeeves, the builder, in 1887. The young couple emigrated to Australia where their daughters were born, but by 1901 they had returned to Hitchin. As the eldest son, he followed his father to head the firm, which he formed into a Limited Liability Company. *"Messrs John Gatward and Sons Ltd were noted as manufacturers of agricultural implements, selling corn and seed drills and under Royal Patronage."* Indeed, the 'Hertfordshire

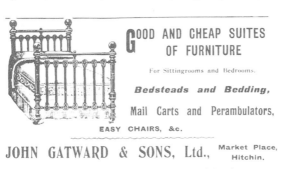

GOOD AND CHEAP SUITES OF FURNITURE

For Sittingrooms and Bedrooms.

Bedsteads and Bedding,

Mail Carts and Perambulators,

EASY CHAIRS, &c.

JOHN GATWARD & SONS, Ltd., Market Place, Hitchin.

A popular cast bedstead design sold by Gatward, Advertisement c.1898 (Hitchin Past and Present, Pat Gadd)

26

Drill', an agricultural seed sower, was a very popular product manufactured, for over 40 years, on the site known as 'Swan Iron Works'. The company also expanded into new areas such as sanitary engineering plus pneumatic and electric bell fitting.

In February 1919 Herbert died, at his home in West Hill, having never recovered from the loss of his 14-year-old daughter some twelve years earlier. His younger brother George took over and ran the company, probably with the help of his elder sister Edith Louisa. He was much more interested in musical activities, however, and the business declined. This might also have been due to the reduction in requirements for agricultural cast iron parts, as tractors and their ploughs, made mostly of steel, took over from horse drawn ploughs. Other founders in the area had enlarged their type of work to include engineering castings (Isaacs), or by specialising in conveyors, sliding doors and heavy lifting gear (Innes), or in steam engines, road rollers, brick- making machinery and eventually diesel engines (Perkins). All of these companies either moved to or were already on a site large enough to permit expansion of their works. These businesses still exist today sometimes with a change of name. The assumed position (See Chapter 6) of the Swan Iron Works foundry, beside West Alley, would not have accommodated enlargement. A second foundry existed in Bedford Street (known as Foundry Street for a short time), old Hitchin maps reveal that it existed in 1881 but had been demolished by 1898. Gatward's had taken on glass and earthenware dealing and telephone installation to augment its range of services but apparently this was not sufficient to halt the decline.

This happened despite the company employing sales staff to bolster business. Mrs Greta Underwood (born in Anderson's Cottages Florence Street in 1921) remembers her father – *"When he married my mother he went to Gatwards - he was a traveller for Gatwards, and it was a horse and cart in those days ... The shop was down at the bottom near the Picture Palace [known as the Electric Theatre] and the Corn Exchange, and the stables were right at the top almost in the [Old] Park Road ... There were several stables at the top of where the Arcade is, and all of these had horses in - no idea who they belonged to. Father's stable was the first one as you went up to where the shops are - it was a slope then - it was the first stable on the right hand side. When I was a little girl I can remember going with my father ... when I was on holiday from school ... and there was his horse. I thought it was wonderful, sitting there watching everything ... One thing I do remember was going up Offley Hill, and I just sort of wondered how the horse was going to manage to get to the top of the hill ... A little while later they swapped the horse and cart for a lorry ... It was so big, open, father learned to drive it."*

No doubt it was his doctor's advice to take things more easily on diagnosing angina in 1923, which influenced George's decision to retire as head of the company late in 1926. His tragic death, 'due to heart failure', took place early on a Sunday morning in August the following year at the old Queen Street Swimming Pool before he could take to the water. The business was already being wound down, prior to his premature demise, the shop in Market Place being converted into the Arcade, which opened in May 1927.

So although the ironmongery and foundry business has long since disappeared, you now know how the Gatwards occupied sites on two sides of Market Place for more than ninety years.

Advertisement on metal plate on the back wall of The Bell Inn, Benington (Richard Whitmore 2005)

Visit the Swan Ironworks

Here we are in Market Place; now cast your eyes over the façade surrounding the Arcade entrance, which Gatward modified to become his 'General and Furnishing Ironmongers' shop. Its large windows, with specially cast iron frames (the first floor ones, although altered, survive to this day), would have displayed many products, mainly household goods and equipment made from iron. On the pavement in front, larger cast items and agricultural implements would be exhibited, especially on market days. Furnishings were fittings of any kind, especially articles of furniture within the house or any incidental part like door handles and locks, sometimes referred to as door furniture. So it was a hardware shop selling products manufactured by others as well as those made at the works in Swan Yard close behind, and West Alley near by.

In these works founding took place where items, from kitchen ranges and stoves to ploughs and rollers, would have been made by melting cast iron bars and pouring them into a mould to cool and harden. Gatward produced rough metal castings using a mould made from green sand (a moist sand and clay mix) formed by ramming it around a pattern or replica of the object to be cast. The resultant casting would require machining, peening or grinding and finishing to produce a more refined product, hence the engineering skills.

The cast iron process begins with the smelting of iron ore with coke (previously charcoal) and limestone to produce pig iron ingots, so called because of the way they appear to be suckling the runner or 'sow' from which they are removed. Re-melting the pig iron with scrap iron in a blast furnace, where air or pure oxygen is blown into the bottom of the chamber, causes a chemical reaction reducing the carbon content as the material moves downwards. The resulting molten liquid is moulded into a bloom or bar which we call cast iron.

Other metals may have been manipulated such as copper, zinc, brass and especially wrought (meaning worked) iron. So the iron works might have included a forge or smithy where heated metal could be shaped by plastic deformation – hammering. Indeed the word 'smith', derived from the word 'smite' – to hit or strike – describes many metal working trades. Hence it follows Black, White, Gold, Silver, Copper, Pewter and Tin and it also

Market day display of agricultural implements outside Gatward's Ironmongery, c.1893
(A Brief History of Hitchin Markets & Fairs, Anthony Foster)

reveals makers of Locks, Blades and Guns – too much wordsmithing here, so here's the exception – 'brazier' meaning brass worker!

Cast and wrought iron have different characteristics derived from their manufacturing methods. Cast iron has excellent machinability and wear resistance and, despite a tendency to be brittle, it has become an engineering material with a wide range of applications including pipes and machine parts. Wrought iron, having a very small carbon content, is malleable and ductile, and was used where a tough material was required such as rivets, chains, railway couplings, water and steam pipes, horse shoe bars, handrails and straps for timber roof trusses etc. This explains how Gatward was able to produce and offer for sale many metal-based products, including sophisticated reaping and mowing machines, as well as venturing into the fields of gas, hot water and steam fitting. Both materials have been replaced to a very great extent by mild steel, a far superior material. An improved process for producing this was invented in 1858 by Henry Bessemer, born locally in Charlton. Thus nowadays wrought iron should in reality be called wrought steel.

So, having observed the shop front, let's walk through the Arcade with its cast iron and timber framed glazed roof support, where Gatward may have displayed furniture, upholstery and bedding, and round to West Alley near to which you can see the vitrified bricks sparkling light off the back wall of the Arcade shops. (See photographs on pages 68 and 69 of the bricks and of Gatward's works viewed from Paynes Park.).

Perhaps we are on the site of Gatward's iron works (with the foundry to the north and forge to the south of West Alley). Imagine you are seeing the red hot metal and quenching steam, feeling the dirt floor and searing heat, hearing the din of hammering and grinding, smelling the acrid fumes and sensing the frenetic founding, forging, fettling and finishing around you.

'Mind your backs', you are in the heart of Victorian Hitchin's industrial area!

This horse trough, now in Market Place, was spotted in a local auction catalogue by an "eagle-eyed" Hitchin resident in 1999. It was rescued and lovingly restored by local volunteers and fittingly returned to within a stone's throw of where it was cast. The archaic spelling of Hitchin crops up even today.

Gatwards Trough, Market Place

Chapter 4

WHAT IS AN ARCADE?

So, first - what is an arcade?

No, it's nothing to do with Arcadia! In fact, it's almost the opposite. Arcadia was known, in ancient and more recent times, as a remote and undeveloped part of Greece, in the North West Peloponnese; the haunt of shepherds with their pipes, and the god Pan, ever in pursuit of charming nymphs; the ideal of innocent rusticity, the Eden of the ancient world.

An Arcade, on the contrary, is quintessentially an urban creation. The word is first found in the English language in 1731, but the thing itself is a Roman invention. 'Arcus' in Latin is 'anything bent at an angle (related to the English 'elbow'); a bow, a rainbow, and so an arch.' It is curious that the arch, from which develop the arcade and the vault, and finally the dome, was known to the ancient Greeks, but, it seems, was rather despised as an architectural form. Ultimate beauty to them was in the post and lintel structure, seen at its apogee in the Parthenon.

The Romans, however, great technicians as they were, realised the potential of the arch for both strength and beauty, and developed all its forms extensively; their pioneering use of cement was put to good use here. The freestanding Triumphal Arch is one of their most characteristic structures; leading nowhere, but expressing power and domination, and whose sole function is to provide a setting for the parade of the victor in battle, with all his loot and captives. We see its descendant today in our own Marble Arch, and the Arc de Triomphe in Paris.

More practically, continuous rows of arches became an essential feature of large public buildings, such as the Basilica (Roman Town Hall), which became the model for the earliest churches; you can see wonderful fifth-century examples in Ravenna.

The Romans also used a chain of arches - an arcade - as a feature of their city shopping centres, giving shelter from both sun and rain, and a convenient place for shopkeepers to store and set out their wares. Some of them - Trajan's Market in Rome is an example - were even on two storeys. (It is interesting that the medieval 'Rows' in Chester use the same idea.) In some places they could kill two birds with one stone: the aqueducts for the city provided a ready-made set of arches, for use as shops and cafes. (The Greeks had had similar sheltered shopping colonnades, not based on the arch, but on capped columns; they were called 'stoas' - whence Stoic Philosophy, since Zeno taught in such a stoa.).

From Rome, the idea was revived in Renaissance Italy - Venice is full of splendid arcades - and thence spread to the rest of Europe. The arcade gave elegance and style to the shopping centres of our cities. England, as ever, was rather late to cotton on to the idea of a shopping arcade, although of course a continuous row of arches had long been familiar in the naves of our churches. The meaning of 'arcade' came to mean 'a covered shopping street', whether it used arches or not; the Shorter Oxford English Dictionary gives the following definition:

A continued arch; a passage; a walk formed by a succession of arches having a common axis, and supported by columns or shafts. Also used of an avenue of trees, etc; and of any covered avenue, esp. one with rows of shops, etc, on one or both sides; 1731.

Hitchin's own Arcade follows this definition, with its idiosyncratic use of arches and posts.

"A's an Arcade,
>   *with shops new and smart,*
>   *Here's wishing them luck with the whole of my heart."*
"A Hitchin Alphabet", Hertfordshire Express, 2 April, 1927 (Hitchin Museum)
(See Appendix 1 for the full text of the Alphabet)

Chapter 5

EIGHTY YEARS IN HITCHIN'S ARCADE

The Business Entrepreneurs

The death of George Gatward and the winding up of the company coincided with a new era in Hitchin's trade. Psychologically, the town was ready to move on following the Great War. Severe building restrictions had been in place between 1915 and 1918, materials and labour were short, and the period immediately following the conflict saw economic uncertainty in the construction trade. By the mid-1920s things were improving, house building was under way and Hitchin turned to face the future.

We will probably never know who dreamed up the ambitious Arcade project. Was it stimulated by the arrival of the elegant Arcade in Letchworth Garden City, built between 1921 and 1923, designed by architects Bennett and Bidwell? Our new neighbour was still regarded with suspicion and some derision by market town traditionalists but that would not stop a little poaching! Or was it simply the presence of the fine over-arching Gatward canopy?

What is certain is that in November 1926 a group of well-respected local businessmen set up a company, "Hitchin Arcades and Developments Ltd", with nominal capital of £8,000, a goodly sum in those days. Their primary objectives were to *"acquire and develop freehold and leasehold properties in the town of Hitchin and elsewhere"* and to *"improve, manage, cultivate, develop, exchange, let or lease, or otherwise, mortgage, sell..."* The project was born.

Of the six Directors, four would have been recognised as stalwarts of the local community. Arthur Lindsell was a solicitor, William Willmott a successful builder, Herbert Marshall Gilbertson a surgeon and Maynard Tomson an estate agent. The remaining two "names" were farmers, Hubert Hailey and Jeremiah Inns. By the 31st December, money was running out and the Inns farming family "obliged" by lending a further £4,500 at 1%. We are reliably informed that the Inns were extremely shrewd businessmen, having founded their prosperity on the sale of hay to the Army!

Four months later, in April 1927, the project came to fruition and the Arcade was open to the public. August 1927 witnessed the conveyance of land in West Alley to Hitchin Urban District Council for the construction of Public Toilets, bringing in a further £200.

Scrutiny of the H.U.D.C. Rate Books and other sources suggest that occupation of the retail units was immediate, although newspapers of the time reported a phased occupation with shops in the Arcade trading before Arcade Walk was fully completed. The venture had achieved its objective and the founding company went into Voluntary Liquidation.

By 1930, a new company "North Herts. Property Development Ltd." owned and managed the Arcade and their name appears in the Rate Books until the early 1960s.

This harmonious and very convenient state of affairs lasted a long time. Sons followed fathers into shops and management decisions were made on site. The Rate Books show that the *"North Herts. Property Development Ltd."* maintained an office above Arcade Furnishers for many years.

A change of company ownership came in 1962. Maynard Tomson, acting for North Herts. Property Development Ltd, briefly entered into negotiations with a London company, but fortunately a syndicate of tenants of some of the Arcade shops was formed and they became the preferred purchasers. The current company "Hitchin Arcade Ltd." was established. As Adrian Pomfret remembers, *"It came up for sale; I think a London company was interested in it and the owners came along and said, "If you can match the offer, we'd rather it stayed local", and that's what happened."*

Times change. In the early days the Company Directors were on site daily, running their businesses. Retirements meant new tenants and added complications. Gradually management moved 'out of house' and into the capable hands of Messrs John Shilcock Chartered Surveyors, located just down Bancroft, and a Hitchin presence since the 1860s. In fact, we are obliged to Mark Seaman-Hill of Shilcock's for his help in clarifying details of the Company's history.

As the Arcade celebrates its eightieth birthday, it is gratifying to note that it still remains a truly <u>local</u> enterprise.

The Changing Face of Trade

"Absolutely the place" (Mrs Beryl Church)

"Since the opening of The Hitchin Arcade a few weeks ago, it has proved one of the centres of attraction and interest for townspeople and visitors. The scheme is as yet, incompleted, although its progress does not impede the business life, which is already in full swing in the Arcade. More shops are to be built and a touch of the picturesque will be added by the garden and shrubbery which are to be provided. Hitchin people are unanimous in their appreciation of another shopping area where the goods are displayed to excellent advantage in attractively designed shops." Bedfordshire Express, 14 May, 1927 (Hitchin Museum)

When the Arcade opened in 1927, Hitchin had a population of between thirteen and fourteen thousand folk. The town had a special atmosphere, with the general Market taking place in Market Place, and on Tuesday there was the cattle, sheep, pig and poultry market in Paynes Park. At this time, of course, the car was not a matter of major concern. Birch Brothers buses were part of the town scene, and LNER could give you a good Whitsun train trip: to London for 4/- (20p), Southend 6/10d (34p) or Skegness 5/- (25p). In 1924 Hitchin had its first motor fire engine.

An important part of Hitchin's history in the 1920s is recorded on the steps of St Mary's Square that tells us of the 1925-29 Queen Street demolition scheme. This saw 174 cottages and yards demolished and 637 inhabitants re-housed. Thankfully Sunnyside and Westmill estates were being built!

By May 1927, ten shops had opened in the Arcade. Also, on the Market Place corner of the Arcade (site of the old Swan Inn), Peark's grocery shop, part of a nationwide chain of 823 shops, started trading. This convenient way of shopping under one roof was highlighted in the advertisements in the Hertfordshire Express dated 14 May 1927.

Ladies were well served. Douglas Moore had a *"Capital selection of coat-frocks, costumes, coats and choice gowns also... is the last word in charming lingerie"*. The shop of Ellen Burges had *"season's models in lovely colours"* and hats were *"available at modest cost"*.

"The well-dressed woman must need to think of another vital item - her hat, or rather hats... They are well-displayed in the soft and lovely colours which are a feature of the season's modes..." Hertfordshire Express, 14 May 1927 (Hitchin Museum)

A wide variety of other goods were also available.

Mr W E Linfield, a practical watchmaker and jeweller, had "prices within the reach of all. There are watches, clocks, jewellery, and plate ... Repairs of any description by skilled workmen." Hertfordshire Express, 14 May 1927 (Hitchin Museum)

Phone
Hitchin 130

Electrical Engineer and Contractor

H. H. BUCKLAR

Specialist in Country House Installations
Lighting, Heating, Power, Bells, Telephones

Any Set
Supplied
on Easy
Terms -

Everything Electrical.
Accumulators Re-Charged.

Estimates & Advice Free - 30 Years' Practical Experience
Authorised Agent for

"Brandes" and "Pye" Products.
Photographic Dealer.
Agent for "Ensign" & Kodak Cameras & Films.

Wireless
Sets and
Loud
Speakers

THE ARCADE
HITCHIN

Advertisement from the Hitchin Directory, 1931
(Hitchin Museum)

"At H.H.Bucklar's is seen a large selection of "Ensign" cameras (and accessories) which will interest the many amateur photographers of the district. There are also wireless sets for the home and portable wireless sets for the picnics." Hertfordshire Express, 21 May, 1927 (Hitchin Museum)

"V is for Valves
for your Radio set.
Mr. Bucklar will tell you the best kind to get."
"A Hitchin Alphabet", Hertfordshire Express, 2 April, 1927 (Hitchin Museum)

Derek Wheeler recalls his aunt, Mrs Bucklar, telling him that her husband had worked in the office at Gatward's Ironworks; he was a pioneering radio amateur and when the Arcade was opened, he set up a radio shop in No.3. China and glass were provided by M.E. Burrows and Mr G. Griffin's shop had a large display of fruit, vegetables and flowers. Mrs Yeo had a toyshop and also a circulating library. In the late 1930s the Countryside Library opened in No.9 The Arcade.

Rodney Wray remembers that in the very early days there were gates at the bottom of

NOTICE

HITCHIN ARCADE LIMITED
as the owner of the thoroughfares
and open spaces adjoining and
adjacent to these buildings gives
notice that they are private property
and all public access continues
only so long as the owner,
Hitchin Arcade Limited, permits.

Hitchin Arcade Limited has not
dedicated and does not intend
to dedicate as a highway the
said thoroughfares and
open spaces or any part
thereof or any way thereon or
thereover.

BY ORDER OF THE DIRECTORS
HITCHIN ARCADE LIMITED

Recent confirmation of the private status of the Arcade (Chris Parker, 2005)

the Arcade. *"They used to be shut once a year to keep it a private right of way … onto the Market Square"* because of course, the Arcade and Arcade Walk are, and have always been, private property. West Alley is the ancient public right of way. However, the public's right of access was extended in 1927 with the sale of land for building Public Conveniences: *"…a right of way for the Council and all persons permitted by it on foot between the hours of Nine O'clock in the morning and Eight O'clock in the evening (except on Sundays, Bank Holidays, Christmas Day and Good Friday) to and from West Alley…through the Arcade to and from the Market Place and a like right of way to and from all parts on the South side of said land…over the Arcade to and from West Alley and the Market Place"* (Conveyance, 14 August 1927)

The upper part of the Arcade (Arcade Walk) evolved later in 1927 and G Launder (outfitters), Ernest J. Harrison (confectioner),

Stanley Chapman (photographer) and Cakebread Robey & Co (ironmongers) moved in. Information gathered from Cakebread's company records shows that this old established (1882) firm moved into No.8 Arcade Walk in 1927 and stayed until 1934. As ironmongers and builders' merchants, they possibly hoped to fill the vacuum left by the disappearance of Gatwards. Cakebread's continues to trade today in Enfield as a multinational company in the supply and distribution of sanitaryware, plumbing and heating materials. They have a small museum at their head office in Enfield that has directors' reports recording the shop in Hitchin.

Over its 80-year existence as a shopping area, the Arcade has seen many businesses change and because of its prime site within the town, the shops are seldom empty for very long. Once we opened the floodgates of memory, images of times and traders from the past 80 years rushed in like a great tidal wave!

The Arcade, looking east, in 1931. The buildings are little changed from how they appear today, but in the foreground there is a fine floral display, including planters and a plinth. They are there no longer, but after the plants were removed, the base of the plinth could be seen for some years, before that too disappeared. (from a contemporary postcard)

How to organise this chapter? Almost impossible! Many businesses have become like old friends, with us over many years. Others have been and gone in an instant. If we have failed to mention an old favourite, or if you wish to be reminded of the overall picture, turn to the Appendix at the end of the book, where our intrepid researchers have attempted an overview of 80 years of occupation. Here we have highlighted a selection of trades and traders, firstly in the Arcade and Arcade Walk, then in West Alley.

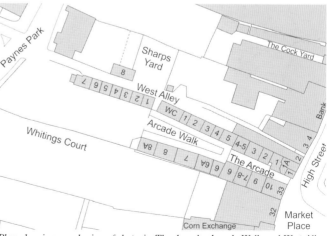

Plan showing numbering of shops in The Arcade, Arcade Walk and West Alley (based on the Ordnance Survey map with the sanction of H.M. Controller of Ordnance Survey)

"Under the drier…"

One profession that has remained in the same area is ladies' hairdressing (No.5 and for a long time Nos.3 and 4 The Arcade). Owners have changed over the years and so, too, have the names over the door. Since 1933 we have seen Anne Duffus, Michael Sinclair, Marion White, Fringe Benefits and lately, Le Folic.

Earlier, in 1927, Miss Hilda Reed had opened her shop at No.7 The Arcade.

Miss Hilda Reed's "is a popular rendezvous with the ladies, now that woman's 'crowning glory' has to be shingled or permanently waved", *Hertfordshire Express, 14 May 1927 (Hitchin Museum). Later she moved her shop to Brand Street.*

Joan Armstrong (née Seymour) remembers the early 1940s:

"Before we left the Grammar school, we had to stand outside Miss Chambers' office and tell her what we wanted to do. I duly went in with everything shaking; she was very stern. "I'm going to be a hairdresser, I'm going to Anne Duffus in the Arcade". I hadn't been at Anne Duffus's more than 2 weeks when - "Joan, would you please go in and put the cape round Miss Chambers?" I nearly died. I had to undo her bun at the back of her head and let down her white hair and comb it out. It was quite long, nearly to her waist. I was really terrified. The most awful experience of my life at the time."

The job, of course, was highly skilled.

"In due course you were taught how to do shampooing. We had models - a sort of wig on a stand or block. We had to practice doing sets and waves; we made a wave and put a comb in to push it up. We did "pin curls"; so different these days. Perms were horrendous, really, weren't they? Everyone was sort of "wired up" to the ceiling on these machines. It took hours to do; the whole morning was taken up doing one person's "perm". It cost 2 guineas for the "ends" and £3.00 for the "full head"; it lasted months!"

Pamela Lockhart (née Reed) worked in the salon at the same time as Joan Seymour, staying there until the early 1950s. *"I was supposed to go to Hilda Reed in Brand Street but was "poached" by Anne Duffus who looked at my hands and said "good hard-working hands; when would you like to start? Saturday?" I got 15/- a week, less a "stamp". National milk cocoa as I was under 15! Anne Duffus found me a really old 'sit-up-and-beg' bicycle with a dress guard. It had 28" wheels; you could really get some speed up. We used to pluck eyebrows, and do manicures while the lady was sitting under the drier. I would sit on a stool and do her manicure; not like today, just a basic manicure. We had a very good class of clientele as you can imagine. The farmers' wives would come in on Tuesday and I remember a Mrs Dudley who wore gaiters. We had some charming people… some not so charming: "I don't think you've rinsed me enough." Younger women - secretaries - came after work on a Friday night. We worked very late on a Friday."*

Meanwhile Janet Hamilton (née Brown) was busy earning pocket money and gaining "work experience": *"In the late 1940s at the age of 14 and whilst still at school, I worked on Saturdays for Anne Duffus at her hairdressing salon in the Arcade. Being very junior and unqualified, my work consisted of assisting the hairdressers, answering the telephone, shampooing clients, sweeping up the hair and generally keeping the salon tidy. This experience stood me in good stead when I left school at 15."*

Janet qualified as a hairdresser, and eventually established a mobile hairdressing business.

Hermann Sander also began his career with Anne Duffus: *"I started at Baxter's in 1957 which was then trading as Anne Duffus. Marjorie Baxter was "The Boss". Miss Baxter always wore a hat, she was the old school and I always stood to attention! In her heyday she was, I believe, what they called a 'Court Hairdresser' and worked for Royalty. I was only 20 and two more chaps came after me. When Miss Baxter sold out, it was taken over by Michael Sinclair. I worked with them until 1960 and then started on my own. I had an agreement that I must not start within a 5-mile radius for 3 years after leaving; in those days you had this sort of agreement and you honoured it. I went to Luton which was very different, so when the 3 years was up, I left Luton and went down to Sun Street and later to High Street."*

In all these years, imagine how many people have had their hair done in the many salons that have thrived here. How many people have been served by all the hairdressing assistants that have made this area so successful under so many names! (Indeed, some of these "assistants" succeeded in running their own businesses after such a good start, for example, Hermann in Sun Street and later at Moss's Corner, Claire Headland in Bucklersbury and Joan Armstrong with their own salons, and Janet Hamilton (née Brown) with her mobile service.). Certainly, some of our strongest memories come from the hairdressing sector, spanning the years.

"Best foot forward..."

Shoes, and feet, too, spring to mind. The Cash & Co Boot and Shoe shop was listed in 1927 at No.2 The Arcade. Miss Tansley, known to many as Mrs Kath Dean opened at No.2 The Arcade in 1939/40. She, and Miss Worbey were both chiropodists, and together with Scholl's Foot Comfort are remembered gratefully by many! Mary Bradbeer (née Upchurch) remembers the 1950s-1960s when *"My father was a regular customer in the Arcade. He was injured in the*

Inside Pomfret's shoe shop showing a cast iron Gatward pillar 2006 (Carola Scupham)

foot during the First World War and had treatment by Miss Worbey, the chiropodist in Scholls."

But of course to many of us "Arcade" and "feet" are synonymous with Pomfrets and Wrays (the latter we will meet in West Alley). For many years the Pomfret family has been in the forefront of the shoe trade in Hitchin. Their shop has sold high quality footwear for both men and women and has been a truly family affair; in fact three generations have served the town.

They started in No.6 The Arcade in the early 1940s and by 1948 had moved into No.9. They expanded into the flagship Arcade shop, 33 Market Place, in the early 1970s. In the 1990s they moved to No.8 The Arcade, after Mrs Beryl Church retired from her pet food business. Many older Hitchin residents will remember that in the early days of the shop they had one of the X-ray machines which were used to ensure that children had the correct size of shoe!

Janet Cleverly (née Terry) came to work at Pomfrets in 1962, aged 15. She was only too eager to leave school where she was told, *"You'll never hold a job down"* - she was naughty at school! And she was still there - over 40 years later. She remembers how they used to pop in to each other's shops for a chat in those days. Most shops shut for lunch at that time and as she lived in Walsworth, she often went to her Nan's who lived in the Churchyard, opposite the old St Mary's School.

E. C. POMFRET
AND SON

for
Good Shoes
BY THE BEST MAKERS

Agents for
K. GOLD CROSS, CHURCH'S,
CLARKS, BREVITT,
SWAN & HEALTH, NORVIC

Children's Shoes
KILTIE, CLARKS, BASIC

Bootees and Slippers
MORLANDS GLASTONBURYS,
JAEGER, etc.

Football Boots
MANFIELD HOTSPUR

All Fittings checked by X-ray

9 The Arcade, Hitchin, Herts
Telephone : HITCHIN 1278

Pomfret advertisement that appeared in the Hitchin Directories 1950s - 1960s (Hitchin Museum)

"Something for everyone..."

Many people have given us their recollections from the past 80 years. One of the most memorable shops during that time was W.H. Church (Nos.7 & 8), a seed and pet food store. Beryl Church ran the shop for 15 years after her husband, Bill, died and it was incredible how much stock was displayed in such a small area. The shop had helpful assistants and was always busy. It had a unique smell, which was evident to everyone who walked up the Arcade, and this is still remembered today. One has to wonder how many tons of seed potatoes were sold from there over the years! Church's traded from the late 1940s until the early 1990s, and the business is remembered with great affection.

Next door to Church's, at No.6, was Wilman's which sold art accessories, pictures and models. At Christmas it was every boy's dream to watch the model train running around in the window. Percy Wilman is listed as a tenant of No.6 in 1937 and is described as "Picture Framer". However, it was not this aspect of the business that set boyish pulses racing! Colin Bates was around in 1959: *"My main memory of the Arcade is that of Wilman's shop at*

"It was a very busy little shop and very intimate in many ways. We always had people that loved growing and needed lovely things to put in pots or their gardens or for their pets. That shop was absolutely full and 4 garages further up the Arcade were also full of stock." (Mrs Beryl Church)

Church's advertisement 1962 (Hitchin Official Guide)

For all . . .

GARDEN REQUISITES
AND
PET REQUIREMENTS

W. H. CHURCH
THE ARCADE · HITCHIN

the top left and the new model railway equipment plus the second-hand equipment in the side window. This window faced Paynes Park, was about 15" wide and 45" tall, as a very rough estimate! I ogled it, aged 8 onwards and frequently spent my pocket money there, perhaps two shillings for a coach."

Nigel and Kathy Freeman take up the story:

"About 1978 we took over the Model & Art business, Wilman's, from Mr R Bird, who told us that the Wilmans had founded it 40 years ago. I spent a week with Mr Bird learning the ropes and was then all on my own. We ran the business for about 8 years, during which time we had some very interesting experiences.

"One day, a very tall dignified man came in. He selected a quantity of art materials which added up to quite a sum. He then found he had no money and said, "Never mind, I will just go to my bank and get some. My name is Lord Lloyd" (Lloyds Bank). He duly came back and paid in cash.

"On another occasion we had a nice young man, who bought several items and paid with a Coutts & Co cheque, on the Windsor Branch. I noticed his name was Bowes Lyon. It turned out he was a nephew of the Queen Mother. On another occasion we had a client, a Mr Waddington, who bought a lot of expensive model railway for his son. My assistant, Jeff, was serving him. He paid with a Coutts cheque for over £100 (this was a lot of money in those days). Jeff asked him for his cheque card. Mr Waddington asked

The
HOME
of
HOBBIES

★ *Picture Framers*

★ PRINTS
★ ARTISTS' MATERIALS
★ STOOLS, SEAGRASS
★ SMALL IRONMONGERY
★ LAMP SHADE MATERIALS
★ MODEL AIRCRAFT
★ TIMBER, PLYWOOD
★ STRIPWOODS, DOWEL RODS
★ ETC. - ETC. - ETC.

THE ONLY SHOP OF ITS KIND DON'T MISS
US WHEN YOU ARE IN HITCHIN AGAIN

WILMANS
(PARTNERS: O. P. & E. A. WILMAN)
ARCADE · HITCHIN, HERTS.

Wilman's advertisement from the Hitchin & Rural District Guide, 1953. The same shopfront still exists (see photograph in Chapter 6)

him what a cheque card was. At this point I interrupted and told Jeff that a Coutts cheque was guaranteed for a quarter of a million pounds.

"One night, around 2 am, we had a phone call from the Police who told us to hurry down and bring our Wellingtons as our shop was flooded. When we opened the door there was 2" of water in the shop and water pouring from the ceiling. A plumber who was working in the shop next door had cut through a pipe and, due to the age of the buildings, they all sloped to our shop so we got all the water."

The model shop trade took a dip in the mid-1980s so the Freemans made the decision to go into ladies' wear and "Scruples" was founded. However, they soon moved their business to Letchworth and to the newly-opened Galleria in Hatfield.

No.6 became Colroy's fruit and vegetable shop and eventually Orchard House, which continued until 1996. It is now occupied by Woodland Interiors.

A succession of greengrocers have been 'in residence', both in the Arcade and in Arcade Walk since 1927: Cecily Edith Griffin, Alfred Moule, Tomlin's and in West Alley, Mrs Ellen Haw and Bob Gates.

H. Tomlin's in Arcade Walk, run by Ted and Alf Tomlin, was the best known.

Colroy's advertising on a brown paper bag

"TRY GRIFFINS"
For Finest Quality

FRUIT
VEGETABLES
FLOWERS
SEEDS

Prices to suit all pockets. Orders promptly delivered

All Floral Designs made to order at the shortest notice on the premises

❀ ❀ ❀ ❀

G. W. GRIFFIN

6, The Arcade - - - Hitchin.

Agents for COOPERS noted Bedford Seeds

"Flowers and fruit in all their glory adorn the window of G.W.Griffin's... and all orders are promptly delivered." Hertfordshire Express, 14 May 1927 (Hitchin Museum)

Orchard House was the last greengrocer's in the Arcade. Brian Worbey named the shop after his grandfather's house. He remembers when a tarantula type spider crawled out of a banana box from an outside display and made its way into the middle of the Arcade. It was spotted by two ladies from Boots the Chemist who were buying fruit for their lunch. Brian collected the spider in a box and teasingly showed it to the ladies of the hairdresser's who were by this time barricading their door and screaming. However, the gas used to spray into the bananas for transport soon had an effect and the poor spider expired, much to everyone's relief.

Brian also remembers a heavy storm one Wednesday morning. *"Rainwater was flooding from Arcade Walk into the Arcade. At the time, the only solution lay with Larry Garnish who lifted the manhole cover, allowing as much water as possible to*

Ted Tomlin talking to Mollie Hancock outside his green grocer's shop, 1981 (Vi Lewis Collection/Terry Knight) and a local press advertisement.

★ FRUIT
&
NUTS ★

CAN HELP TO MAKE YOURS
A HAPPY
CHRISTMAS.

Call and see our selections of the best quality Fruit and Nuts.

H. TOMLIN & Sons

THE ARCADE :: HITCHIN

drain away before all the shops down to the Book Bug were flooded."

Brian's shop had one customer who came in twice a day and helped herself to stock without paying. This was "Wigsy", a lovely Jack Russell terrier owned by Julie from Oh La Di Da. Wigsy used to come in for her Bonio and attention; she was one of the Arcade's characters.

An earlier much-loved character was "Rusty", the Arcade cat. Marjorie Barrow recalls that *"he was a beautiful cat that was befriended by most of the shopkeepers - Crone's the furnishers and the coal office among them - as well as the car park attendant. In the end, his little body was found on a roof in Brooker's Yard; he must have toiled up the fire escape to sleep, at night. A Hitchin Worthy - if on <u>four</u> legs!"*

By 1937 Countryside Libraries Ltd. had opened up at No. 9 The Arcade. Mary Bradbeer (née Upchurch) was a keen customer: *"I first joined the public library in Brand Street but found it very intimidating; the librarian was elderly, in a long black dress, and you just dare not make a noise as there were SILENCE notices on display. When the Countryside Library opened in the Arcade, where Pomfret's shop now is, I joined. I believe it was 2d each visit. They had a wonderful selection of children's books, and all my favourite Chalet School series."*

Pansy Mitchell (née Wells) was also a patron, as were her parents: *"The library was owned by Mr Don Smith... Mum knew him and was often first to get the new books ... mysteries or 'Westerns' for Dad. The children's books! There was a wonderful selection! There were two I used to get out time and again, which used to make Mum cross, as it was about 3d a week. One of them was called "The Lord's Prayer" ... I can't remember much about it now!"*

*Wigsy, 1995
(Brian Worbey)*

*Rusty the ginger
cat; Arcade
resident, owner
unknown 1981
(Marjorie Barrow)*

Next door at No.10, and later round in 33 Market Place were J.A. Pirkis, Decorator's Merchants, remembered by Pansy Mitchell for the samples of wallpaper which revolved on a cylinder in the side window - innovative for the 1940s! In the late 1970s, part of No.10 was made into a staircase for offices above 33 Market Place; the remainder was incorporated into 33 Market Place.

Another Arcade Walk shop in the 1940s and 1950s was the open-fronted Harry's Cut Price Groceries, with a roller shutter. The proprietor, Harry Lewis (Vera Lynn's brother-in-law), went on to buy a ladies' fashion shop under his wife's name (Sara Lewis) - now Starbucks coffee shop in Market Place. In fact, grocers occupied this particular shop from 1933 until the mid-1960s - first Sidney Fox, next Harry's Cut Price, then Murray's, which gave way to the redoubtable Phil Stone, a true Arcade character, remembered with great affection by many.

Phil Stone is remembered for nearly always having a smile on his face and for being immaculately turned out as befitted the master tailor he was. He was also a Chairman of the Arcade Company and became involved in the saddlery business that was situated in Arcade Walk during the 1970s. His tailoring business was listed at 1a The Arcade in 1937 and he remained there until the mid-1950s, then moving to No.1 Arcade Walk. By 1960 he was at both No.1 and No.3 as "Tailor and Outfitter". 1973 saw his change of direction as "The Arcade Saddlery" was established in Nos. 2 and 3, where it was listed until 1981. His sewing machine remains above the shop to this day!

*Wooden coat
hanger with
Phil Stone's
nameplate
(Simon
Walker)*

Other names from the past evoke memories. Rodney Wray remembers The Record Shop run by Mr Lawrence, listed between 1948 and 1979: *"Mr Lawrence sold records in quite a plain shop, as you could only buy 78's and sheet music in those days. Everyone who went in to buy a record had to cut their way through the smoke because he was a chain-smoker."*

However, not everybody was granted satisfaction! Pansy Mitchell remembers: *"Mr Lawrence had a "short fuse"! I'd left school and I was in the Letchworth Ladies' Choir. I ordered some sheet music from him which he said would be in on the Wednesday. I went in on the day and he shouted at me because he said I had come in too early! I never went there again."*

Pansy also had a mortifying purchase at Rennette's Ladies Wear (No.3 The Arcade, 1948-1960): *"I'd just started work. I bought a red corduroy coat there, which was my pride and joy. Mum and I had gone on a coach trip to Clacton for the day, on Birch Coaches (5/-, 25 pence!). It rained ... my coat got wet, the colour ran, my flowery dress was dyed red! It never washed out."*

Research into shop-keeping is a source of constant delight. Two intriguing tenancies of Arcade Walk in 1937 spring to mind. Frank Hawley Clarke, Dog Breeder, occupied No.1a. The imagination boggles! We have a better idea of trade practices a little further up Arcade Walk. Rodney Wray's father remembered a chap who did signwriting in a shop before the war and then got on to signwriting by post. Sacks and sacks of mail turned up with postal orders and money. It was the first time his father had seen someone light a cigarette with a £1 note, but the chap disappeared because he did not keep up with answering his mail.

Wright and Geary (later The Arcade Furnishers Ltd.) had well over 40 years of trading. The tall John Wright and his sister were popular figures on that side of the Walk, and the business progressed to carpets, rugs and mats together with new beds and furniture. Beryl Church recalls: *"John Wright was quite a character. He used to hang his rugs all along the Arcade. That was how he used to display his wares; it was a big chunk of the Arcade."*

Brian Worbey and Chris Parker discussed the history of the business (1937-1981) with Claude and Pat Geary and say:

"A great many people can remember one side of the Arcade being taken up by the Arcade Furnishers Ltd (Wright & Geary) and this is really a North Hertfordshire success story.

Claude's father, William T Geary, started in the trade in 1921 in Baldock. In the 1930s Mr Wright Senior, having failed with a business venture in Letchworth, went to work for Mr Geary. The business progressed and a shop was opened in Bucklersbury, Hitchin. Mr Geary's son Claude came into the equation, helping to sell second-hand furniture in Hitchin. Claude remembers being involved with the Hitchin Thespians by

This photograph of Arcade Furnishers Ltd also shows the remains of the plinth from the Rose Garden in the foreground (Claude Geary)

supplying them with furniture for props for their shows in the Hermitage Cinema."

"They moved into No.10 The Arcade in 1937, and Mr Wright's son and daughter, John and Catherine, joined the business. In 1938 Arcade Furnishers was founded and they expanded into Nos. 6,7 and 8 Arcade Walk, taking up one side. They sold mats, carpets, rugs, furniture and beds - anything to do with the house. The company were proud to say, "order on a Saturday morning and we will deliver Saturday afternoon." There's service for you!

"The shop in the Arcade continued to sell furniture until 1981. We are pleased to say Claude and his wife Pat are still trading in Baldock as Geary's, and still seem to get a buzz from the business."

1952 Receipt with obligatory stamp – a method of raising revenue before VAT!

"Battening down the hatches": the Arcade at War

As elsewhere in Hitchin, the wartime economy called for discipline amongst the traders. Able-bodied men (and women) joined the services, leaving gaps to be filled by those left behind. Claude Geary joined the RAF, John Geary went into the Army. Both were away for the duration, as were others. Derrick Else recalls a chance encounter with one Arcade shopkeeper: *"Circa 1943/44, after moving up and down North Africa, I went to RAF Telecommunications at Heliopolis, Cairo. There, behind the counter in the camp post office I met a chap called Lawrence, previously the proprietor of the record shop at 1, The Arcade and from whom I had purchased a Benny Goodman long-playing record."*

Rationing and shortages with the dreaded "coupons" restricted the activities of food and clothing shops. It was the "make do and mend" era.

Up at the hairdresser's they were "doing their bit". Joan Armstrong (née Seymour) explained:

"I had to make the shampoo. It was awful green soft soap, which we had to have during the war because there wasn't very much to choose from really. You spooned it out and added water. Then you had to stir and stir until it all dissolved. Then you had a liquid goo. We had to put it into stainless steel mugs, one in each cubicle."

This was not the only hardship. Joan and her friends were "fire-watchers", constantly alert to danger from the skies: *"During the war we had to have fire-watching. Miss Duffus used to do it but she said, "Joan, do you want to do the fire-watch for me?" Miss Jenkins who also worked for Anne Duffus, Miss Tansley who had the Chiropodist's shop on the corner, and I had to do the fire-watch once a fortnight. We had to go and sleep in the shop at the top which is now a wool shop in West Alley. Fortunately it was towards the end of the war when there weren't any fires! What we'd have done if the siren had gone off - I wasn't sure what we were supposed to do anyway! We slept on these camp beds at the back of this shop and in the morning we used to go down to our shop. Fortunately we'd got a customer who kept chickens and they let us have some eggs. We had a boiled egg in our shop, boiled up in the saucepan we boiled up the shampoo in!"*

Then, at work, there were other difficulties: *"Power cuts caused problems, as in those days even perms had to have electricity. Say a power cut was scheduled from 12pm to 2pm; we used to get all the customers lined up to go under the drier ready to go. I'm sure we used up far more electricity than they saved having the 2-hour power cut!"*

"Changing times ..."

A massive change of ownership happened at the beginning of the 1980s, with the retirement and closing down of Tomlin's, Phil Stone and Arcade Furnishers. The furnishing shop became Milligan's, a cafe with a Western Style Restaurant upstairs, which caused quite a stir in the town.

Phil Stone's shop (Nos. 2 & 3) became Hitchin Heating & Bathroom Supplies and Davis and Jennings (Domestic Electrical). William Jennings, who was a good friend of Phil Stone, has a fund of amusing stories about life in the Arcade area during the 1980s. William formed a partnership with Bill Davis who owned a shop in Walsworth Road, and they traded together at No. 3 Arcade Walk for 5 years as Davis and Jennings. One weekend he went away, leaving Bill to look after the shop. Returning on Monday, William asked how trade had been in his absence.

"It was wonderful, the first time we had that type of restaurant in Hitchin. He opened quite late and did late meals. It was an absolutely going enterprise. He was fired with enthusiasm; he'd just got a certain something - a very great charisma. It was so busy and he was a character. He started with tables outside and it looked nice; the food was good and then in the evenings he opened again." (Beryl Church)

47

Numbers 7 & 8 Arcade Walk opened with J.R. Car Radio and Bee Video Systems, shown here with cycles in the cycle rack. The garages in the background have now been demolished

"We had a good weekend, and I sold the washing machine." "What washing machine? NOT the one I brought in for repair…?"

Number 5 (formerly Tomlin's) was for a short period Breaker 19 (CB Radios), a revolution in communication, particularly between long distance lorry drivers. From 1982 until 1999, Arcade Reproductions took over. The owners were John and Jenny Banham, now the proprietors of Merrick's sweet shop in the High Street at the entrance to the Arcade.

West Alley

For the purposes of this chapter, we have treated West Alley as a separate entity, simply for convenience. However, there is a significant difference between it and its neighbours. The alley itself is an ancient Public Right of Way leading from the west into the heart of Hitchin. It was never, like the neighbouring Arcade, part of the "Swan Inn" or its yard.

The area, which is now a car park for the disabled, was once occupied by a row of cottages, "Sharps Yard". Rodney Wray remembers: *"There were 7 houses with an entrance yard. You went through an alley and there was another yard at the back. Mr Bates used to live there and there was a step where a*

An old metal street sign in West Alley 2007 (P. Douglas)

dog used to sit - with his backside on the step and his front feet in West Alley watching the traffic go by. The cottages were demolished in 1958."

Many remember the Antiques Market set up on the site in the 1960s by the Market Superintendent, Gilbert Day. It flourished until the 1990s. Judith Wray recalls that *"West Alley Antiques Market was held Tuesdays and Saturdays. I used to have a stall on a Tuesday. Every stall was taken and there was a wonderful selection of antiques. The dealers from London and American shippers would arrive early to find any good buys as the stall holders unpacked and set up their wares. Many of the stallholders went on to run shops and trade from Woburn and antique fairs."*

Beryl Church also remembers Alfred Cottages, facing Paynes Park and demolished in 1966:

"There were 3 cottages opposite the Library with a shed at the bottom where Mr Martin used to keep bikes. Everyone had bikes in those days, not cars. He used to sit at the entrance to his shed and by 8.00 o'clock in the morning it was full of bicycles from Pirton, Shillington and all round. They were just stacked; how he got them out at night, I don't know. He charged 6d a week to look after your bike. The ones who did not pay left their bikes outside, those who did pay could use the shed."

A whole chapter could be devoted to West Alley! Shop units opened here from the 1930s. To many, the Alley will always be

WEST ALLEY ANTIQUE MARKET

Open: Tuesdays, Saturdays and Bank Holidays

Antiques Bought and Sold

Silverware - Jewellery - Copper and Brass
Furniture - China - Glass - Postcards
Basketware - Books, etc

W.I. home-made produce on Saturdays

Refreshments available

Advertisement for West Alley Antiques Market in the Evening Post Echo supplement, 'Hitchin Past & Present', December 1977 (Brian Worbey)

associated with the Wray family. In 1930, the young Charlie Wray had to get special references to open his shop as he was under 21 at the time. The shoe repair trade (with 50% contract work including Police & Fire Brigade footwear) was so busy at one time that Mr Wray and his work force took up 5 units! Mr Wray's son, Rodney, worked with his father

A **'GOOD** Cup of Tea ; Meal ; Service can be **ASSURED**

WHEN VISITING

THE "ARCADE" CAFÉ

OR THE

PAYNE'S PARK CAFÉ

HITCHIN.

Moderate Charges.   Civility Always.
OPEN SUNDAYS.

Try us for Pure Ice Cream in the Summer !
THE OLDEST ESTABLISHED IN HITCHIN.

Proprietor: A. BROLIA.

An advertisement for Brolia's Café

and later took over the business. He remembers that everyone knew everybody in those days. They used to do small jobs for nothing for regular customers, but in the end, overheads were such that they had to charge for everything.

One of young Rodney's early jobs was as Company tea boy: *"In the 1950s, Brolia's cafe (Paynes Park Café) was where Stapleton's is now. The buses used to park in Nuns Close and the drivers and ticket ladies would get out and have a cup of tea or a "full English" in the café. One of my first jobs, even though I'd been to the Grammar School, was to go and fetch the tea … take an enamel jug that tall up to Brolia's, with all the orders for rolls, buns … Any boy who started in our place, that was his first job … lunch time and tea time. They were Italian and made ice cream!"*

He recalls that Wray's used to repair bags, harnesses, straps, leather belts and had all the latest machinery. Welted shoes had the soles sewn on and shoe repairers within a 20-mile radius used to bring in shoes to have the soles stitched. On Tuesdays (Market Day)

AGRICULTURAL COUNTRY BOOTS, SHOES AND WELLINGTONS

WRAY'S HITCHIN
(Shoe Repairs)

2-6 WEST ALLEY
THE ARCADE
Tel. HITCHIN 4776

Advertisements for Wray's show the wide range of services they provided (Rodney Wray)

WRAYS
OF HITCHIN LIMITED

Engraving on the premises.
Trophies and Tankards
Printing and photocopying.

2-6 West Alley, The Arcade, Hitchin
Tel: Hitchin 4776

they had sackfuls of shoes to have the soles stitched, and this took all day. It went on into the early 1960s when Doc Martin's and Tuf shoes meant the beginning of the end for the shoe repair trade as they knew it.

By 1937 The Ministry of Labour had established an Employment Exchange in West Alley, taking up 3 units. Our records show that they were still there in 1941. Those seeking work used to queue up to go in and Rodney recalls that the queue would stretch past Wray's shop: *"They used to watch the men working inside. The benchmen used to work in the window so they could get maximum light; less spending on electricity because you used to think of these things in those days!"*

Rodney eventually retired in the mid-1990s. At this time his wife, Judith, had already started the Willow Room, specialising in home interior accessories. This business is still going strong in West Alley today, although in a slightly different form.

In the late 1940s, Ken Logan (later to become a District Councillor) shared a shop with a Mr West, repairing radios and clocks, before moving his business to Grove Road, then to Bucklersbury, and lastly into Bancroft.

Adrian Pomfret recalls: *"When we went into 33 Market Place, we stopped using No.1 for storage and it was just sitting there. My mother and Pat Lambourne decided to open it up as an Antiques Shop ... It took over their lives."*

The Willow Room

5 West Alley, The Arcade,
Hitchin, Herts. SG5 1EG
Tel: 0462 434776

JUDITH WRAY
Basketware, Furnishings & Flowers

Willow Room business card (Judith Wray)

Charrington's Fuel Office occupied No.7 West Alley for around twenty years from the early 1970's. Previously the premises had been the home of J. O. Vinter & Son Ltd (Fuel Merchants). This price list, with two magnificent draught horses, dates from 1986.

Acorn Antiques were at No.1 West Alley for many years.

51

"At Your Convenience"

Reference has been made to the conveyance by "Hitchin Arcades & Developments Ltd" of a piece of freehold land in West Alley to Hitchin Urban District Council for the construction of Public Toilets. The conveyance document, dated 4th August 1927, states *"The Council shall with all convenient speed erect on the land coloured pink on the said Plan a Public Convenience ... and shall at its own cost and to the reasonable satisfaction of the Vendor erect a proper end wall to the adjoining building on the East. All entrances from the said Public Conveniences onto the Arcade shall be provided with iron gates and keys of such gates shall be provided for the use of the Vendor. The Vendor reserves a right to run a covered glass way along the south side of the said Public Convenience."*

Amazingly, memories of these particularly useful additions to the Arcade have been difficult to access! Rodney Wray remembers a blue internal decor, but as a young lad thinks that his attentions would have been directed elsewhere. Derrick Else recalls in the 1960s that: *"Tony King was the HUDC surveyor. His name, as the responsible official, was beautifully inscribed in the Gent's lavatory."* Pamela Lockhart admits *"... they were there, but we walked past them quite quickly. They were reasonably respectable."*

1927 rainwaterhead on the wall in West Alley near to the original entrance to the public conveniences (K. J. Fitzpatrick-Matthews, 2007)

More positively, Pansy Mitchell remembers that the entrance was originally in West Alley and that *"they were spotlessly clean and NEVER smelt!"*

In 1960, plans were drawn up by Martin Priestman, an architect based in Churchyard, for "The Hitchin Arcade Scheme". This included the trelliswork that remained on the southern aspect of the public toilets until the major refurbishment by North Hertfordshire District Council in 2007.

"You don't realise it has changed so much!" (Beryl Church)

Few things illustrate the changing face of Arcade trade better than a trawl through the Commercial Rate listings of the shops. The 1930s, represented by milliners, costumiers, wireless and drapery shops, have been superseded by our lingerie, fitted furniture and Body Magic Health Salon, by way of C B radio and a video shop.

The "flagship" shop, 33 Market Place, has over 80 years, been occupied by Pearks'

Stores, Provident Clothing and Supply Company, Pirkis and Son, Decorators Merchants, Walpamur, E.C. Pomfret (footwear), House of Flowers, and now O2 Phones. And of course, before any of these, The Swan Inn, now long forgotten.

Many Arcade and West Alley occupants have gone on to find larger premises: South East Security, Denis Howard ("The Clockman") and Just Lace for example. Pauline Cronin, the proprietor of Just Lace, started business in the Corn Exchange, and after her stint in Arcade Walk moved to premises in Bancroft, where she renamed her shop Not Just Lace.

Shirley Avery (née Davies) took over from Lay's in 1986 and sold everything that tea and coffee connoisseurs could possibly want. In 1993 she expanded into larger premises across Arcade Walk so her loyal customers could also sit and enjoy a cuppa. Her eventual move to larger premises in Market Place made her 'Tea & Coffee House' a trademark for the town. For others, the intimate experience of Arcade trade has been just right and they have flourished, leading to continuity and some very longstanding shops such as The Book Bug (Tom and Sue Jevon), A Touch of Garnish (Larry and Elaine Garnish), Nips & Tucks (Pam, Christine, Robyn and Merlin, no less than four generations of the Clarke family!)

How gratifying it is to see that after 80 years of history, the Arcade is still managing to offer a unique and varied shopping experience for the people of Hitchin and visitors alike.

No chain stores or supermarkets here!

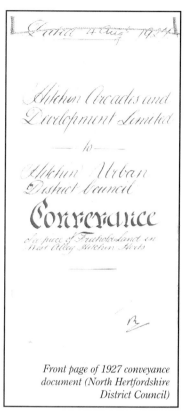

Front page of 1927 conveyance document (North Hertfordshire District Council)

"Although not within the Arcade, Messrs Pearks' stores have been erected as a result of the Arcade scheme.... Messrs Pearks' have 823 shops throughout the kingdom... they buy on a vast scale and are able to sell best quality goods at low prices." Hertfordshire Express 14 May 1927 (Hitchin Museum)

A compliment slip from the Tea & Coffee Shop. (Shirley Avery) Hatters continues in this premises.

Howard's needed more space and relocated to Baldock. Advertisement from Evening Post Echo, December 1977 (Hitchin Museum)

Postscript

Time does not stand still. Even as we go to press, changes are taking place. During the summer of 2007, the row of garages, so fondly remembered by Beryl Church, were demolished. At the same time, North Hertfordshire District Council carried out major renovations on the public conveniences.

The wooden garages, shown here in 2005 (K. J. Fitzpatrick-Matthews)

Chapter 6

BRICKS, BEAMS AND GLASS

The Arcade today consists of diverse buildings, erected at different times and altered through the years to produce what can be seen today. This is a good reminder that we do not live in a museum and never have done: we humans are creatures who constantly change the world around us, including the buildings in which we spend so much of our lives. It also makes this description a mere snapshot. Within weeks of this book being printed, elements of the buildings will have changed and, over time, previously hidden elements will be exposed, parts that exist today will be lost, new sections will be added and so the process of change, which we call history, will carry on.

With this important proviso firmly in mind, we can examine the structures currently on the site to see what evidence they hold for their history. We know from documentary evidence summarised in the previous chapters that the Arcade as we now know it was created in 1927, its official opening taking place on 17 May

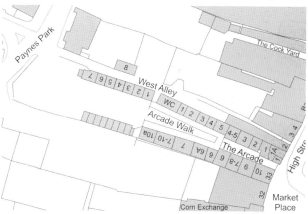

Plan of the buildings today (based on the Ordnance Survey map with the sanction of H.M. Controller of Ordnance Survey)

(although Reginald Hine incorrectly states that it opened in 1928). Before this, it had been the yard and display area for the ironmonger John Gatward & Sons and before 1884, it had formed the yard of The Swan Inn for at least three hundred and fifty years. As such, it was just one of a number of yards that led west from High Street, Market Place and Bucklersbury. With West Alley (formerly Post Office or Cod Piece Alley), it is a main pedestrian route from the town centre through to the Library and Museum, linking Market Place with Paynes Park, along a gentle rise of around 3.6 metres (about 11 feet 10 inches).

The buildings that exist today can be divided into two main groups: the Arcade proper, which is the part covered by a glass roof, and Arcade Walk, which is the part with a

A view of The Arcade from a tower crane in 2005 (© Chris Titmus)

colonnaded walkway. There are some other structures, too. West of Arcade Walk is an area used as a car park and, on the north side, the backs of a row of early twentieth-century buildings fronting West Alley. Until July 2007, there was also a group of early twentieth-century garages on the south side of the car park. They were used as lock-ups prior to their demolition. The site contains mostly commercial premises, with seven shops in the Arcade and nine in Arcade Walk; it is also the location of the most central public toilets in the town. There is a uniformity of design to the buildings, extending down to details such as the glazing bars and panelling of the doors, which has been kept by more recent additions (the public toilets from c 1927 and 8A Arcade Walk from 2004).

The Arcade

The Arcade is approached through a broad carriageway, with two chambers above (shown on earlier photographs as one chamber with a dormer in the roof space above it). Although the entrance today is open, a photograph of c 1894-1900 (the whole photograph is seen on page 25) shows massive, studded timber gates, also visible on an older photograph of The Swan (see frontispiece). The style of the gates suggests an early sixteenth- or even late fifteenth-century date. They are probably contemporary with the construction of No.10 The Arcade/No.33 Market Place, the timber-framed Swan Inn (see below).

Inside Gatward's yard from Market Place (Hitchin Museum)

In its present form, the Arcade was created to display large iron goods made by John Gatward & Sons, as shown by historic photographs; the work may have taken place shortly after the acquisition of the former Swan Inn by John Gatward in 1884 or it may be slightly later: the Ordnance Survey map of 1881 shows Swan Yard without roofing, while the 1925 edition shows it roofed. It has generally been supposed that the present roof was added c 1884, but the photograph of c 1894-1900 shows it without the west wall pierced with three arches, and it has a plain panelled glass canopy quite unlike the present complex roof. On the other hand, an advertisement of 1902 (see page 26) shows the present roof in place, with a gallery at the west end over doors with glazing panels where the three arches now stand open. The buildings themselves are of brick (although those toward the street frontage enclose timber framing, early sixteenth-century in the case of No.1 and possibly late fifteenth-century in the case of No.10) with old tiled roofs to the south and slate to the north.

Inspection inside the shops was carried out in May 2006, which revealed details not visible from the outside. The shop fronts are not on their original lines, but have been extended about a metre into the former yard; the original front wall of the upper storey has been retained, supported on cast iron columns, some of which are stamped with the name

Gatward (see drawing page 39). These support a
lintel (possibly also cast iron) that is not visible in
any of the premises at present. Above the lintel, a
narrow crawl space has been created in front of
the old wall, accessed by the original window
openings. Most of this work precedes Gatward's
late nineteenth-century alterations, as the
extended frontage to all but Nos.5 and 6 is already
present on the 1851 Board of Health map; it does
not appear on Henry Merrett's map of 1818,
though. It must therefore be a development of
The Swan Inn before the fire of 1853, again raising
the question of how much damage it caused. As
John Gatward did not begin his ironmongery
business until 1835, this narrows the date further.
The cast iron column inside No.5 has an ornate
capital, quite different from the plain forms to the
east; it is clearly of a different date, which the map
evidence shows to be later, and possibly dates from
the time of Gatward's purchase of the property in
1884. It could have been part of the work
undertaken to cover this part of the yard.

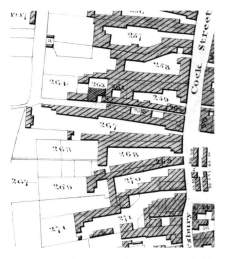

*Detail from Henry Merrett's 1818 map (Hitchin
Museum). 267 is Swan Yard*

*Detail from
the 1851
Hitchin
Board of
Health map
Note Alfred
Cottages at
left end of
Swan Yard
(Hitchin
Museum)*

The present roof is a complex wood, iron and glass structure, which closely resembles the roof of the Corn Exchange, designed to allow as much light as possible into the Arcade. It is supported on seven wooden trusses with iron ties and braces. They hold up a lantern running the length of the roof with panels of four panes of glass and a pitched slate roof, hipped at the western end. The panels can be opened by means of a screw mechanism operated from wheels above the shop fronts. The strengthened glass panels that are the main source of light are hung from the lantern and do not rest on the trusses; at the bottom, they are laid on the flat roof of the crawl space with lead flashing top and bottom. This structure is shown on a photograph of c 1902 and the similarity of its construction to the roof of the Corn Exchange, which was replaced c 1895, suggests that it dates from roughly the same time. It is possible that both were made by the same company; whether the ironwork was produced by Gatward or by Thomas Perkins (also of Market Place) is not clear.

The roof structure, looking towards Market Place (K. J. Fitzpatrick-Matthews)

One feature of the buildings that is not apparent from inside the Arcade is that there is a change in the rooflines between the Arcade and Arcade Walk. However, it does not coincide with the west end of the Arcade but lies further east, between Nos. 4 and 5 on the north side and between Nos. 6 and 7 on the south. The roof of those buildings at the eastern end of the Arcade is lower and on the north side it is composed of slate and less steeply pitched. The roof abuts the gable ends of the higher roofs of Arcade Walk. On the south side, the ridge line of the Arcade's roof lies noticeably to the north of that for Arcade Walk by about a metre. This change marks the point at which the 1835-1851 forward extension of the frontages ended.

*The change in roof lines, seen from
the north (K. J. Fitzpatrick-Matthews)*

Beneath No.6 The Arcade, there is a cellar, reached from a staircase between this property and No.6 Arcade Walk. Its walls are composed of nineteenth century brick, although the brick floor may be somewhat earlier. In the northwestern corner, a slightly sunken area is probably a sump for water leaking into the cellar; within it, a low pedestal once held a cast iron stove. There is a small cast iron door in the wall behind where the stove stood. The joists supporting the floor of the shop above appear to be a twentieth-century replacement. The position of the staircase, against the outside of the end wall of the Arcade, suggests that the cellar existed before Arcade Walk was constructed. We will discover when that happened later, but it confirms that this was the cellar of the Swan Inn, at least during the nineteenth century.

Arcade Walk

Arcade Walk did not exist in its present form until the formation of the Hitchin Arcades and Development Company in 1926 and the conversion of the Arcade into individual shop units in 1927; indeed, it was not opened until a few months after the Arcade. Unlike the Arcade, its frontages maintain the original line of the stables shown to be here on maps up to 1881. They have late eighteenth-century coloured brickwork (red stretchers and purple headers to create a chequered effect) to the front, while the rears are of plain brickwork. The gable end of the north range has a concrete plaque inserted just above the level of the flat roof of the public conveniences, reading "Hitchin U.D.C. | own the whole of | this wall | 1927", which presumably records the conveyance of the land on which the toilets stand to the Urban District Council on 4 August 1927.

Although there is an overall unity of style, there are nevertheless differences between the north and south ranges. The most obvious difference on a plan of the site is that the south range is rather deeper than the north. The south range has roof skylights that appear to be original features (one, over No.8, has been filled in), whereas only one shop in the north range has a skylight, which is clearly a late twentieth-century insertion. The trusses supporting the roofs are identical in form throughout each range, but differ between the north and south. The windows to the upper floors are of similar design in both ranges (small wooden casements of three by two panels), but those in the north range are different in detail from those in the south.

Both ranges have been much altered. The stairs appear to have been inserted, rather than being integral to the original construction. This was perhaps done when the former yard was acquired by John Gatward, as the mouldings appear nineteenth-century, rather than when Arcade Walk was created in the 1920s. The shop window frames are of the same design as those in the Arcade, as are the doors (apart from a few that have evidently been replaced), but these are more in keeping with late 1920s styles.

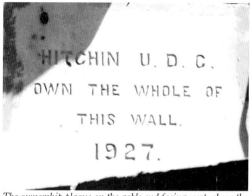

The ownership plaque on the gable end facing west, above the Public Conveniences: seen from the car park for the disabled that was once Sharps Yard (K. J. Fitzpatrick-Matthews)

There is a wood and glass canopy in front of the shops, which does not appear on the 1925 Ordnance Survey map and which must therefore have been erected for the creation of Arcade Walk in 1927. However, much of the wood in the construction seems to be of more recent date (perhaps as late as the 1980s), as are the gutters, which are plastic, in contrast to the cast iron down-pipes. Arcade Walk was refurbished in 1960, so some of the alterations could have occurred then, although this is probably too early for the use of plastic drainpipes. Beneath many layers of paint, a florid G or C within a rose can still be seen moulded in the brackets supporting the down-pipes: are they Gatward products? It is evident from these details that the history of this canopy is not straightforward.

The G or C monogram on a drainpipe (K. J. Fitzpatrick-Matthews)

The area in the centre, which is raised at the east end, was originally planted with roses, as shown in a photograph of 1931 (see Chapter 5). The planting is thought to have served as an advertisement for Harkness Roses, established near Hitchin by 1895 and in Walsworth in the 1920s.

The detail of the design of many doors has not changed since 1927 (K. J. Fitzpatrick-Matthews)

The type of roof truss in the northern range (K. J. Fitzpatrick-Matthews)

One of the most intriguing differences between the two ranges of buildings lies in the two distinct styles of roof truss that cannot be explained by the different depths of the ranges. Those on the north side consist of a massive horizontal tie-beam (the bottom chord) with cross braces to the top chords, which support the rafters with clasped purlins. The joints are numbered with Roman numerals, an indication that they were manufactured off site, disassembled and coded for reassembly on site.

The trusses on the south side have a set of vertical posts above the even more massive bottom chord, while the first floor is supported on massive beams, not present in the northern range. These differences are consistent along the lengths of the ranges, from those elements of these ranges now enclosed within the Arcade to the western end of Arcade Walk, but both sets are massive and relatively roughly finished, on a scale that seems completely out of place for such presumably lowly structures as these. Nevertheless, they are not obviously re-used from other

Detail of Roman numerals for assembling the trusses in the northern range (K. J. Fitzpatrick-Matthews)

buildings and argue for a unity of design within the ranges. This poses problems for the interpretation of the north range, where there is evidence for at least three separate periods of construction, as will be explained below.

The type of roof truss in the southern range (K. J. Fitzpatrick-Matthews)

One aspect that is not immediately apparent is that there is a faded painted design on the frontage of the south range that survives only at first floor level, especially visible over No.8, but also present on No.7. It clearly predates insertion of the first floor windows, which cut into the design. It survives only above the level of the canopy, which indicates that it must be earlier than 1927. The content of the design is no longer obvious, although it appears to consist of florid lettering in white, with pale blue 'shadows' to give a three-dimensional effect. Whether it is connected with Gatward or with The Swan Inn or some other business in Swan Yard, such as Kershaw's coaches, is not at all clear. The letters on No.8 may originally have read "& Co", but it is not possible to deduce what the remainder might have been.

Preserved below the canopy to No.8, there are traces of two flattened brick arches, now largely hidden by the wooden panelling of the nameplate of the shop front. One is above the present door, but the other lies immediately to the east, indicating that there were formerly two doors or one door and an open arch to this unit. This might indicate that it once served as a smithy, not unreasonable in an inn yard.

The faded design over No.8 Arcade Walk (K. J. Fitzpatrick-Matthews)

Public conveniences *(see opposite page)*

The public toilets at the western end of the north range was erected in 1927, as shown by a cast-iron rain head on its north wall (see page 52). An attempt was made to match the detailing of its brickwork with the historic fabric of Arcade Walk, although it was given a flat roof rather than pitched. They were originally serviced along a corridor running between the gents' and ladies' lavatories, accessed by a door in West Alley, which is now blocked; later, the service entrance was through the gentlemen's lavatory. The wooden trelliswork across the frontage was put on in 1960. Plans to upgrade the facilities were put forward by North Hertfordshire District Council in 2006 as part of an overall revamping of public toilets throughout the district and at the time of writing, the work is under way.

1 The Arcade/1 High Street

This building is clearly jettied, with each floor oversailing the one underneath, as can be seen from the street frontage. The present whitewashed façade, which dates from the eighteenth or early nineteenth century with modern shop fronts, conceals a timber framework, parts of which are still visible inside. In 1759, the Trustees of the Hitchin to Bedford Turnpike purchased and demolished a butcher's stall on the north side of The Swan gateway to improve access. This must have been in the form of a pentice or lean-to added to the front of 1 High Street. No trace of it survives in the visible fabric.

10 The Arcade/33 Market Place

As discussed in the chapter on The Swan Inn, it became evident during the site inspection of May 2006 that considerable elements of the timber framework of The Swan survived the fire of 1853. Historic photographs do not help in understanding the framework, as the building was refronted in brick some time before 1840, long before the first photographs were taken of the town. Samuel Lucas's sketch *Supper at The Swan* of 1845 shows a beam, on which a sporting gun and other objects are hung, together with a series of joists running from it and wooden floorboards (see page 15). There may be a brick fireplace to the rear. It is not clear how accurate a depiction of the room the sketch is, as Lucas's interests were directed more toward the characters of the diners than toward architecture. Although The Swane is first recorded in the early sixteenth century, it is possible that it was built by The Brotherhood around the time of its foundation in 1475. Indeed, the style of the gates still in place shortly before 1900 is in keeping with a late fifteenth-century date.

The chamber immediately over the carriageway has a beam supporting the floor above with a rounded moulding. This matches a moulding on the curved beam itself supporting the chamber and is again of late fifteenth- or early sixteenth-century type. A chamber in this position would have been of high status and would have been reserved for wealthier patrons, if not the innkeeper himself. The room above has been considerably modernised, as have all those fronting Market Place, although original details may well survive.

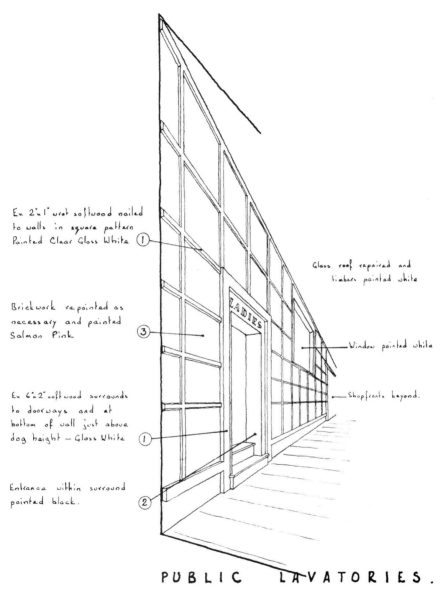

Ex 2″×1″ wrot softwood nailed
to walls in square pattern
Painted Clear Gloss White ①

Brickwork re-painted as
necessary and painted
Salmon Pink ③

Ex 6″×2″ softwood surrounds
to doorways and at
bottom of wall just above
dog height — Gloss White ①

Entrance within surround
painted black. ②

Glass roof repaired and
timbers painted white

LADIES

Window painted white

Shopfronts beyond.

PUBLIC LAVATORIES.

*Architect's drawing of proposed changes to the Public Convenience in
1960 by Martin Priestman, BArch ARIBA. (Rodney Wray)*

In both this property and No.1 The Arcade/No.1 High Street, a series of interesting
nineteenth-century fittings has been preserved. These include a fine brass cupboard door
catch, stamped Ashwell's System (a similar item from Edinburgh was auctioned on eBay in

October 2006 and was sold for the princely sum of £16!), and lavatory fittings (a cast iron cistern reading "The Storm King" leaves the imagination reeling: was this another Gatward product?).

The moulded beam, a survival from The Swan Inn (K. J. Fitzpatrick-Matthews)

Charming, ornate cupboard door latch (K. J. Fitzpatrick-Matthews)

The Storm King (K. J. Fitzpatrick-Matthews)

West Alley

Evidence on the rear of the north range of The Arcade/Arcade Walk

There are a number of changes in the brickwork forming the north side of Arcade Walk facing West Alley that suggest different phases of building, which at first sight appears to contradict the evidence of the roof trusses. There are straight joints in the brickwork in three places: between the public conveniences and No.1 Arcade Walk, 9.5 m east of this (between Nos.2 and 3 Arcade Walk) and 8.5 m east of that (between Nos.4 and 5 Arcade Walk). It may safely be assumed that the earliest phases lie to the east and the latest to the west, but there is no trace of these changes on the south side, where the shop fronts are now, nor inside the buildings. However, the roofline is roughly level from No. 5 Arcade Walk eastwards, whereas it is rather sinuous to the west, showing a change in the nature of the ridge at that point. This would then have to be the earliest part of the buildings. It has bricks that seem to be intended to measure 8¾" × 4" × 2½" (the examples measured are in the range 215/220x105x60/65 mm).

The next unit west (Nos.3 and 4 Arcade Walk) has a blocked up window about 0.55 m wide and 1.9 m above ground level in what is roughly the middle of No.3. The bricks here seem to have been intended to measure 8½" × 4" × 2¼" (measured examples are in the range

215/220x100x57mm). West of this, Nos.1 and 2 have a blocked up doorway 1.1 m wide somewhat left of centre; this would have given access to No.2. The doorway was evidently altered at some point during its use, as the blocked portion is beneath a wooden lintel that does not quite match the position of a flattened brick arch above it. This part is shown as a single unit on the Board of Health map of 1851. The bricks in this unit were evidently intended to measure 8¾" x 4¼" x 2¼" (the measured examples being in the range 225x110x60 mm).

The blocked window to No.3 Arcade Walk (K. J. Fitzpatrick-Matthews)

A view of the north wall of Arcade Walk, showing variations in the brickwork (K. J. Fitzpatrick-Matthews)

The blocked doorway to No.2 Arcade Walk (K. J. Fitzpatrick-Matthews)

While these pieces of evidence for a sequence of building do not seem to be matched by the evidence on the south side of the range (although the southern wall of this range was not available for inspection, and this is where we might expect to find such evidence), they point to the growth of the inn yard during the later eighteenth century; all the structures in The Swan Yard shown on the 1851 map appear in the same positions on Merrett's map of 1818, while the map of the town recently shown by Bridget Howlett to date from 1736-72 and perhaps to be a product of William Willmoor in the 1750s or 60s shows at least one range. If we accept this range to be the southern, we have a date of construction for that range of before c 1770 (and perhaps a considerable time before), and for the north range of 1770-1818. The unity of design of the roof trusses in the north range can then be explained if we assume the original roof to have been a victim of the fire of 1853 (its east end adjoins John Gatward's property) and the present roof trusses to be their replacement. The brickwork of the shop fronts suggests a complete refacing at some point in the decades before 1800.

Another feature of the north wall of this range is traces of industrial activity in the brickwork, most noticeably the vitrified bricks that appear along much of the wall. Bricks vitrify under high temperatures, over around 1850° C (the precise temperature depends on

Part of the map of 1736-72 attributed to William Willmoor (now in Hitchin Museum)

the chemical composition of the clay from which the brick is made). For the bricks on this wall to be affected in this way, there must have been something reaching a very high temperature nearby. While it is possible that this "something" was the fire of 1853, another possibility presents itself: a nineteenth-century photograph shows the west end of West Alley, with 7-8 Paynes Park visible on the left hand side and the currently derelict 'barn' (No.8 West Alley, dated 1749 from incised bricks on the east gable) just beyond the garden

Vitrified bricks on the north wall of Arcade Walk (K. J. Fitzpatrick-Matthews)

wall of the house. An industrial structure is visible ahead, with the legend GATWAR[D] on a painted sign; this is clearly a blacksmith's shop or forge in which Gatward & Son were making some of the items sold in their shop at the front of the Arcade. In the narrow gap between the former building and Arcade Walk, it is possible that there were vents and chimneys blasting out air hot enough to vitrify the bricks in Arcade Walk. Almost opposite, further east on West Alley, the 1851 map shows a 'Smithy and Iron Foundry' that was presumably connected.

There were other significant buildings in West Alley. A Society of Friends' Meeting House was built on the north side in 1694, although the Quakers had a new Meeting House built in Brand Street in 1838. The first bank in the town, The Hitchin Bank, founded c 1780, lay in the house of its director, a Mr Everitt, in West Alley and soon moved to Cock Street, occupying the site where Barclay's Bank now stands.

Alfred Cottages (so named on the Board of Health map of 1851, but also wrongly recorded as Alpha Cottages in the census returns of the same year – the maps are bound in

West Alley from Paynes Park in the nineteenth century (Hitchin Museum)

Hitchin Museum with an incorrect date of 1852) once faced Paynes Park at the western end of what is now the car park. They are already present on the mid eighteenth-century map attributed to William Willmoor and may figure on Drapentier's map of c 1690, published in Chauncy's *Historical Antiquities of Hertfordshire* in 1700. They were demolished during the widening of Paynes Park in 1966.

Alfred Cottages, on Paynes Park, looking north (Hitchin Museum)

Fascinating features to be found in and around Hitchin Arcade (K. J. Fitzpatrick-Matthews & Ian Horton)

Historical importance of the buildings

Although the buildings of the Arcade and Arcade Walk were once listed Grade III, a non-statutory grade that was dropped in 1970, they are no longer listed, with the exception of No.1 The Arcade/No.1 High Street (Grade II). They appear not to have been upgraded to Grade II during the revision of the Hitchin List in 1973 as they were assessed to be of nineteenth-century date, which would not have justified inclusion given the criteria used at that time. This is a pity, as they form an interesting and unusual group. Subsequently, Arcade Walk has been included in The Register of Important Local Buildings for Hitchin, compiled by North Hertfordshire District Council.

However, as this book has shown, there is more to the Arcade than nineteenth- and twentieth-century properties: both buildings at the street frontage retain sixteenth- or seventeenth-century cores, while the buildings of Arcade Walk date from the second half of the eighteenth century, and probably rather earlier at the eastern end of the south side. All of the surviving structures have complex histories that were not appreciated by those who undertook the original listing or the revision of 1973, and which have only become apparent through an inspection of the interiors of each property and through long familiarity with the buildings.

It is now clear that what we have is adapted from what survives of the late eighteenth-century courtyard of The Swan Inn. It has connections with several important local families (the Kershaws, who were landlords in the early nineteenth century, and the Gatwards, who transformed the inn into an ironmongers in 1884) and a recorded history that can be traced back to the Dissolution and beyond. More than that, it is the only surviving representative in the town of a coaching inn courtyard of this date: there are older examples at The George, The Sun, The Red Hart and so on, but none from the last century of the coaching trade, when it was in its heyday. As such, they are buildings that have much to tell us about the history of Hitchin and neatly illustrate changes in its economic fortunes over five hundred years. In short, the Arcade is a microcosm of the post-medieval town.

Appendix 1

Whilst researching this book, contributors discovered this local gem in Hitchin Museum, hidden in the Hertfordshire Express of Saturday, 2nd April, 1927. It is clearly looking forward to the opening of Hitchin Arcade. The poet is unknown, but motoring was obviously at the forefront of his mind.

A HITCHIN ALPHABET

A's an Arcade, with shops new and smart,
Here's wishing them luck with the whole of my heart.

B is a Councillor, weighty and wise,
To arouse us from slumber he certainly tries.

C is a Clyno, a job that's well done.
"See Morgan about it," he'll give you a run.

D is a Dodge, full of dash, full of devil,
The saloon will do "60" - of course, on the level.

E is "Express", full of all the late news,
It allows every party to air its pet views.

F is a Froth Blower - a good idea struck,
To help Waifs and Strays who are down on their luck.

G is a Gadget, that's known as a Gun,
For greasing the shackles - five minutes - they're done.

H is a Hermitage, now being razed,
To make way for the shops that are now being raised.

I Icknield Way, made by Eocene men,
And we haven't progressed so much further since then.

J for the Joy that the Smiling Spring shows,
Though it frequently freezes or blizzes or snows.

K for the Kinship all Motorists feel -
Camaraderie "urge" for the man at the wheel.

L is for Letchworth. Has gained its renown
By having the depot for Fords in the town.

M is a car that there's no need to name,
Real value and merit earned it wide fame.

N is for Norton, the bike, not the place,
It won the T.T. in the Isle of Man race.

O is for Oxford and Cambridge Old Blues,
Or Oxford and Cowley, whichever you choose.

P Preposition, do you say that you will
Go *on* top or *in* top up Bwlch-y-Groes Hill?
(In either case I shan't believe you)

Q is for Queen Street. Improvements are due.
Will the pictures we recently published come true?

R is the Rover, which "runs like a six",
'Phone No.5 Baldock for further parties.

S is the Station a mile from the town,
We could do with a dozen more trains up and down.

T is for Traffic. Now, would the new orbital
Relieve the congestion and really absorb it all?

U for Utility. Sturdy and strong,
The Trojan has never been known to go wrong.

V is for Valves for your Radio set.
Mr. Bucklar will tell you the best kind to get.

W Wolseley, by Morris now run,
Has a top-gear performance that's second to none.

X for X Rays. How nice it will be
When inside the engine we're able to see.

Y for the Youth on the Sports motor bike,
Mr. Chalkley will get any make that you like.

Z for the Zeal which I always display,
In toddling off home at the close of the day.

Appendix 2

THE CHANGING FACE OF TRADE IN HITCHIN ARCADE, ARCADE WALK AND WEST ALLEY (1927 - 2007)

There is a great deal of detail available on the occupation of the shops, offices and buildings comprising the Arcade, Arcade Walk and West Alley since the Arcade was opened in 1927. This documented information has been extracted from:

The Hertfordshire Express and Hitchin, Letchworth & Stevenage Gazettes
Local papers (Hitchin Museum)

Kelly's Directory of Hertfordshire
An annual directory showing a list of businesses throughout Hitchin. This also contained advertisements for those businesses that were prepared to pay. Today this is available as an online version of the long established Kelly's Directory of UK businesses.

Hitchin Directory
A directory of shops, offices, businesses etc providing names and addresses of, amongst other things, the proprietors (Hitchin Museum)

Hitchin Urban District Council Rate Books
Herfordshire Archives and Local Studies, County Hall, Hertford

Goad Plan
From 1885 until 1968, fire insurance maps of urban areas were produced by the firm of Chas. E. Goad Ltd. The Goad Plan is now recognised as a definitive source of information for the retail and property market. It was first commissioned in 1965 by the Department of Trade and Industry, when Chas E. Goad brought together the physical layout of town centres with details of the occupiers and their lines of business. Updated versions are available in a number of formats. (Hitchin Library)

In this book we have distinguished the three principal elements; the 'main' Arcade, Arcade Walk and West Alley as follows:

The Arcade refers to the first section of shops running west from Market Place and covered by the glass roof. In 1927 there were initially 12 shop units and offices, but time has seen some changes. No.1a, above the present 'Bookbug', and originally an Insurance Office, was no longer a separate unit by 1930. Adaptations have also occurred at No.10, with the blocking of an original doorway, and the creation of a new entrance and shop utilising part of No.33 Market Place. No.33 has always formed part of the overall Arcade complex.

Arcade Walk is a new section formed in 1927 and is an extension to the rear of the Arcade. The shops here utilised what were the old stables and yard of the Swan Inn. These shops originally numbered 9 units but were extended to provide a further unit in 2004.

West Alley (its most recent name) was, and remains, an important established public right of way between Paynes Park and Market Place/High Street. Previous titles include Codpiece (or Codpisse) Alley, Quakers' Alley (after the Meeting House established there in 1694) and Post Office Alley (when a shop at its High Street end became just that in 1837). By the early 20th Century it consisted of a row of cottages, Sharps Yard, running at right angles to the main path. These were demolished in 1958. Many remember the Antiques Market subsequently sited here and it is now a car park for the disabled. Alfred Cottages, demolished in 1966, faced Paynes Park at the top of the Alley. West Alley did not form part of the Arcade complex until the 1930s.

The details of the various businesses over eighty years (1927-2007) give a fascinating insight into the changing face of trade.

SHOPS & BUSINESSES: 1927-1930

	1927	1929	1930
Arcade			
1	Herbert Douglas Gamble (Confectioner)	Herbert Douglas Gamble (Confectioner)	Herbert Douglas Gamble (Confectioner)
1a	Royal Mutual Insurance Society Ltd	Royal Mutual Insurance Society Ltd	Royal London Mutual Insurance Society Ltd
2	A. L. Yeo (Books,Library Toys)	A. L.Yeo also Downe & Poole (Statnrs)	Downe & Poole (Stationers)
3	H. Bucklar (Camera & Wireless)	H. Bucklar (Camera & Wireless)	H. Bucklar (Camera & Wireless)
4	Cash & Co.(Boot & Shoemakers)	Cash & Co.(Boot & Shoemakers)	J. G. Saunders Ltd /Cash & Co.Ltd
5	Maud E.Burrows (China Glass Hardware)	Maud E.Burrows (Hardware)	George J. Launder Ltd & Maud Eliz Burrows
6	G.W. Griffin (Fruit & Vegetables)	Mrs Cecily Edith Griffin (Fruiterer)	Misses Rockcliffe & Hudson, Mrs Griffin & Geo Walker
7	Miss Hilda Reed (Hairdresser manicure etc.)	Miss Hilda Reed (Hairdresser manicure etc.)	Miss Hilda Reed (Hairdresser manicure etc.)
8	Miss Ellen Burges(Milliner)	Miss Ellen Burges (Milliner)	Miss Ellen Burges
9	Douglas Moore (Gowns Coat- frocks etc.)	Miss A. B. Ingham (Costumier)	Miss A. M. Fotheringham
10	Wm.E.Linfield (Watches,Clocks Jewellery)	Wm. E. Linfield (Jeweller)	Wm. E. Linfield (Jeweller)
Front 33MP	Pearks' Stores (Meadow Dairy Co Ltd)	Pearks' Stores (Provision Dealers)	Pearks' Stores Ltd
Arcade Walk			
1		B.R. Newberry	B.R. Newberry
2	George J. Launder (Outfitters)	George Launder (Outfitters)	George Launder Ltd
3		Harry H. Bucklar (Electrical Eng & Cont)	British Showcard Service Co Ltd per C H Gilbert & Sons
4		British Showcard Service (Ticket Writers)	British Showcard Service Co Ltd per C H Gilbert & Sons
5	Ernest J. Harrison (Confectioner)	Ernest J. Harrison (Confectioner)	E. J. Harrison
6		Rest Room - Hitchin Arcade Developments Ltd	Rest Room - Hitchin Arcade Developments Ltd
6A	Stanley Chapman (Photographer)	Stanley Chapman (Photographer)	V. S. Baker
7			
8	Cakebread Robey & Co Ltd (Ironmongers)	Cakebread Robey & Co Ltd (Ironmongers)	Cakebread Robey & Co Ltd
West Alley			
1			R. Brown
2			Miss Ebden
3			E. J. Chapman
4			
5			Isaac Hawkins / Barclays Bank Ltd (owners)
6			
7	Note George Walter Griffin moved from Hitchin Hill into No 6 in 1926 (Kellys 1926)		Sharps Yard, 5 dwellings owned by John Brown
Ref.	Hertfordshire Express 1927 & Kelly's Dir	Hitchin Directory & Kelly's 1929	Herts CC Water Rates and charges

SHOPS & BUSINESSES: 1933-1940

	1933	1937	1939/40
Arcade			
1	Miss Marjorie E. Heather (Confectioner)	Mrs Ann Duffield (Confectioner)	Mrs Elsie Lawrence
1a			R. Ellery
2	Provident Clothing & Supply Co Ltd (No No.)	Miss Kathleen Mary Tansley	Miss Kathleen Mary Tansley
3	Francis Productions Ltd (Furniture Manf)	Ernest Leeson (Tailor)	H. W. Bottoms, Miss Elsie Thompson
4	Miss Anne Duffus (Ladies Hairdresser)	Miss Anne Duffus (Ladies Hairdresser)	Ernest Leeson
5	Miss Anne Duffus (Ladies Hairdresser)	Miss A. Duffus (Ladies Hairdresser)	Miss Anne F. Duffus
6	Mrs Minnie Bronia (Refreshment Rooms)	Percy Wilman (Picture Framer)	Percy Arnold Wilman per Messrs Geo Jackson & Son
7		Barty Edwards (Gents Hairdresser) No No.	William Harold Church
8	Miss Ellen Burges(Milliner)	Miss Ellen Burges(Milliner)	William Robinson & Miss Ellen Burges
9	Miss A. B. Ingham (Costumier)	Countryside Libraries Ltd	Countryside Libraries
10	William E. Linfield (Jeweller)	Wright & Geary - The Arcade Furniture Stores	Victor Edwards
Front 33MP	Peark's Stores (Provision Dealers)	Pearks' Stores (Provision Dealers)	Pearks' Stores (Provision Dealers)
Arcade Walk			
1	Mrs Bertram Newbury (Draper)	Frank Hawley Clarke (Dog Breeder)	Frank Hawley Clarke
2	Sidney Fox (Grocer)	Sidney Fox (Grocer)	Soloman Fox
3	G Bucklar & Co Ltd (Electrical Engineers)		John Clements Harvey
4		Marianne - Misses Drake & Harvey Outfitters	Solomon Fox
5		Alfred Moule (Fruiterer) - no number of shop	Jesse Tomlin (Fruiterer)
6			Wright & Geary - Store & Premises/ N. Herts Property Dev. Ltd
6A			John Henry Wright & William Geary T/A Arcade Furnishers Ltd
7		Norman Walton Signwriter (Studio & Premises)	Norman Walton (Studio & Premises) Arcade Registry Office
8	Cakebread Robey & Co Ltd (Ironmongers)		John Henry Wright & William Geary T/A Arcade Furnishers Ltd
West Alley			
1		Ministry of Labour Employment Exchange	H.M. Office of Works for H.M. Labour Exchange
2		Ministry of Labour Employment Exchange	H.M. Office of Works for H.M. Labour Exchange
3		Ministry of Labour Employment Exchange	H.M. Office of Works for H.M. Labour Exchange
4			
5		Charlie Wray (Boot Repairer)	Charlie Wray (Boot Repairer)
6			
7		No Number - Mrs Ellen Haw (Fruiterer)	Mrs Ellen Haw
			3 Houses - 5 Dwellings Sharps Yard Barclays Bank
Ref.	Kelly's Directory of Hertfordshire 1933	Kelly's Directory of Hertfordshire 1937	General Rates/Water Rates

SHOPS & BUSINESSES: 1948-1957

	1948	1949/50	1953	1956-57
Arcade				
1	Elsie Lawrence (Radio & Records)	Elsie Lawrence (Radio & Records)	Elsie Lawrence (Radio & Records)	Elsie Lawrence (Radio Dealer)
1a	Phil Stone (Tailor)	Phil Stone (Tailor)	Phil Stone (Tailor)	J. A. Pirkis & Son Ltd
2	Miss Kathleen Mary Tansley (Chiropodist)	Miss Kathleen Mary Tansley T/A Mrs Deans	Miss Kathleen Mary Tansley (Chiropodist)	Miss Kathleen Mary Tansley (Chiropodist)
3	Rennette (Ladies Coats)	A. Brass - Rennette (Ladies Wear)	Rennette (Ladies Wear)	Rennette (Ladies Coats Costumes)
4	Ernest Leeson (Leather & Fancy Goods)	Ernest Leeson then Anne Duffus Feb 1950	Miss Anne Duffus (Ladies Hairdresser)	Miss Anne Duffus (Ladies Hairdresser)
5	Miss Anne Duffus (Ladies Hairdresser)	Miss Anne Duffus (Ladies Hairdresser)	Miss Anne Duffus (Ladies Hairdresser)	Miss Anne Duffus (Ladies Hairdresser)
6	Wilmans (Art Models Pictures)	Wilmans (Art Models Pictures)	Wilmans (Art Models Pictures)	Wilmans (Art Models Pictures)
7	W. H. Church (Seeds Pet Foods)	William H. Church (Seeds Pet Foods)	William H. Church (Seeds Pet Foods)	William H. Church (Seeds Pet Foods)
8	C. Robinson (Ladies Outfitters)	S. D. Walker	S. D. Walker (Ladies Outfitters)	S. D. Walker (Ladies Outfitters)
9	Ernest C. Pomfret(Footwear)	Ernest C. Pomfret	Ernest C. Pomfret (Footwear)	Ernest C. Pomfret (Footwear)
10	J. A. Pirkis (Decorators Merchant)	J. A. Pirkis & Son Ltd	J. A. Pirkis (Decorators Merchant)	J. A. Pirkis & Son Ltd(Decorators Merchant)
Front 33MP	Provident Clothing & Supply Co Ltd	J. A. Pirkis & Son Ltd	Provident Clothing & Supply Co Ltd	The Provident Clothing Supply Ltd
Arcade Walk				
1	J. R. Farrington "Studio One" (Photographers)	Philip Stone (May 1949)	Philip Stone (Tailor)	Philip Stone (Tailor)
2		Solomon Fox	Harry's Stores (Grocers)	Harry's Stores (Grocers)
3	John C. Harvey (Osteopath)	John C. Harvey T/A J. C. Harvey(London) Ltd	The Palette Pottery	The Palette Pottery
4	A. C. Silk (Fancy Goods)	A. C. Silk (Fancy Goods)	Mrs P. A. Smith (Ladies Outfitters)	Mrs P. A. Smith (Ladies Wear)
5	Jesse Tomlin (Fruiterer)	Jesse Tomlin (Executors)	J.Tomlin (Fruiterer)	J.Tomlin (Fruiterer)
6	Arcade Furnishers Ltd (Wright & Geary)	Arcade Furnishers Ltd (Wright & Geary)	Arcade Furnishers Ltd (Wright & Geary)	Arcade Furnishers Ltd (Wright & Geary)
6A	Arcade Furnishers Ltd (Wright & Geary)	Arcade Furnishers Ltd (Wright & Geary)	Arcade Furnishers Ltd (Wright & Geary)	Arcade Furnishers Ltd (Wright & Geary)
7	Arcade Domestic Agency (V.M. Stannard)	North Herts Property Development Ltd	Arcade Domestic Agency (V.M. Stannard)	Arcade Domestic Agency (V M stannard)
8	Arcade Furnishers	Arcade Furnishers Ltd (Wright & Geary)	Arcade Furnishers Ltd (Wright & Geary)	Arcade Furnishers Ltd (Wright & Geary)
West Alley				
1	West & Logan (Radio & clock repairs)	K.W.Logan	West & Logan (Radio & clock repairs)	E. C. Pomfret (Shoes)
2	Charlie Wray (Shoe Repairs)	Charles Wray	C. Wray (Shoe Repairs)	A. McParland and C. Wray (Shoe Repairs)
3	H. Bates	Stirk Bros Ltd	Stirk Bros & H. Bates	H. Bates
4	J. Williams	Charles Wray	J. Williams	Ada M. Williams
5	Mrs R. Hawkins	Charles Wray	Mrs R. Hawkins	Charlie Wray (Shoe Repairs)
6	William Stone	William Stone (North Herts Property Dev Ltd)	William Stone	A. Stone
7	Hull (Greengrocer)	Mrs Ellen Haw (North Herts Property Dev Ltd)	Bob Gates (Greengrocer)	Bob Gates (Greengrocer)
	Sharps Yard (2,4,5 & 6) names W. Legate, W. J. Baines, A. French & F. Viney .	Sharps Yard 5 Cottages (2,3,4,5 & 6)	Sharps Yard (2,3,4,5 & 6) names R. Brown, Miss L. Roberts, Mrs B. Pilling, A. French & F. Viney	
Ref.	Hitchin Directory 1948	HUDC Rates & Water Rates	Hitchin Directory 1952-53	Hitchin Directory 1956-57

SHOPS & BUSINESSES: 1959-1969

	1959-60	1964-65	1965-66	1968-69
Arcade				
1	Elsie Lawrence (TV & Records)	Elsie Lawrence (Records)	Elsie Lawrence (Records)	Elsie Lawrence (Records)
1a		Scholl's Foot Comfort Service	Scholl's Foot Comfort Service	Scholl's Foot Comfort
2	Miss K.M.Tansley (Chiropodist)			
3	Rennette (Coats & Costumes)		Marion White (Ladies Hairdresser)	Marion White (Ladies Hairdresser)
4	M. Sinclair (Ladies Hairdresser)	Marion White (Ladies Hairdresser)	Marion White (Ladies Hairdresser)	Marion White (Ladies Hairdresser)
5	M. Sinclair (Ladies Hairdresser)	Marion White (Ladies Hairdresser)	Marion White (Ladies Hairdresser)	Marion White (Ladies Hairdresser)
6	Wilmans (Timber Models Pictures)	Wilmans(Artists Materials)	Wilmans(Artists Materials)	Wilmans(Artists Materials)
7	William H. Church (Seeds Pet Foods)	William H. Church (Seeds Pet Foods)	William H. Church (Seeds Pet Foods)	William H. Church (Garden Supplies)
8	William H. Church (Seeds Pet Foods)	William H. Church (Seeds Pet Foods)	William H. Church (Seeds Pet Foods)	William H. Church (Garden Supplies)
9	E. C. Pomfret (Footwear)	Ernest C. Pomfret & Son (Footwear)	Ernest C. Pomfret & Son (Footwear)	Ernest C. Pomfret & Son (Footwear)
10	J. A. Pirkis & Son (Decorators Merchant)	J. A. Pirkis & Son(Decorators Supplies)	J. A. Pirkis & Son (Decorators Merchant)	J. A. Pirkis & Son(Decorators Supplies)
Front 33MP	J. A. Pirkis & Son (oil colour and paint)	J. A. Pirkis & Son(Decorators Supplies)		Walpamur Distributors Ltd
Arcade Walk				
1	P. Stone (Tailor)	Manway Cleaners	Manway Cleaners	Vacant
2	Harry's Stores (Grocers)	Murray's Grocers	Murray's Grocers	Philip Stone (Tailor)
3	P. Stone (Outfitters)	Phil Stone (Tailor)	Philip Stone (Tailor)	Philip Stone (Tailor)
4	Mrs P. A. Smith (Ladies Wear)	Hydes The Bakers	Hydes The Bakers	Hydes The Bakers
5	Tomlin Bros(Fruiterers)	H.Tomlin & Sons (Fruiterer)	H.Tomlin & Sons (Fruiterer)	H.Tomlin & Sons (Fruiterer)
6	Arcade Furnishers Ltd (Wright & Geary)	Arcade Furnishers Ltd	Arcade Furnishers Ltd	Arcade Furnishers Ltd
6A	Arcade Furnishers Ltd (Wright & Geary)	Arcade Furnishers Ltd	Arcade Furnishers Ltd	Arcade Furnishers Ltd
7				
8	Arcade Furnishers Ltd (Wright & Geary)	Arcade Furnishers Ltd	Arcade Furnishers Ltd	Arcade Furnishers Ltd
West Alley				
1	E.C.Pomfret (Shoes)	E.C.Pomfret & Son (Footwear)	E.C.Pomfret (Shoes)	E.C.Pomfret (Shoes)
2	Charlie Wray (Shoe Repairs)	Charlie Wray (Footwear & Repairs)	C.Wray (Shoe Repairs)	C.Wray (Footwear & Repairs)
3	Charlie Wray (Shoe Repairs)		C.Wray (Shoe Repairs)	
4	Charlie Wray (Shoe Repairs)		C.Wray (Shoe Repairs)	
5	Charlie Wray (Shoe Repairs)			
6		West Alley Grill (Restaurant)	West Alley Grill (Restaurant)	West Alley Grill (Restaurant)
7	Greengrocer			J. O. Vinter & Son Ltd (Fuel Merchants)
				Antique Market
Ref.	Hitchin Directory 1959-60	Hitchin Directory 1964-65	Hitchin Directory 1965-66	Hitchin Dir. 1968-69 & Goad Plan Oct 1969

SHOPS & BUSINESSES: 1973-1983

	1973	1979	1981	1983
Arcade				
1	Elsie Lawrence (Radio & Records)	Elsie Lawrence (Records)	Merry Go Round C/WR Toys	Merry Go Round C/WR Toys
1a				
2	Footcare	Footcare	Footcare	Footcare
3	Marion White (Ladies Hairdresser)	Marion White (Ladies Hairdresser)	Marion White (Ladies Hairdresser)	Rite Price Sports
4	Marion White (Ladies Hairdresser)	Marion White (Ladies Hairdresser)	Marion White (Ladies Hairdresser)	Marion White (Ladies Hairdresser)
5	Marion White (Ladies Hairdresser)	Marion White (Ladies Hairdresser)	Marion White (Ladies Hairdresser)	Marion White (Ladies Hairdresser)
6	"Wilmans(Art, Models Pictures)"	"Wilmans(Art, Models Pictures)"	Wilmans(Art & Toys)	Wilmans(Art & Toys)
7	William H. Church (Seeds Pet Foods)	William H. Church (Seeds Pet Foods)	William H. Church (Pet & Garden)	William H. Church (Pet & Garden)
8	William H. Church (Seeds Pet Foods)	William H. Church (Seeds Pet Foods)	William H. Church (Pet & Garden)	William H. Church (Pet & Garden)
9	E. C. Pomfret (Footwear)	E. C. Pomfret (Footwear)	E. C. Pomfret (Footwear)	E. C. Pomfret (Footwear)
Front 33MP	E. C. Pomfret (Footwear)	E. C. Pomfret (Footwear)	E. C. Pomfret (Footwear)	E. C. Pomfret (Footwear)
Arcade Walk				
1	Trinket Trove (Gifts)	Denis Howard (Antiquarian Horologist)	Howard (Watch & repairs)	Denis Howard
2	Arcade Saddlery	Arcade Saddlery	Arcade Saddlery	Hitchin Heating Bathroom Supplies
3	Arcade Saddlery	Arcade Saddlery	Arcade Saddlery	Davis & Jennings (Domestic Electrical)
4	Hydes The Bakers	Vacant	Breaker 19 (CB Radio)	Edge (Ladies Wear)
5	H.Tomlin & Son (Fruiterer)	Tomlin & Son (Fruit & Veg)	Tomlin & Son (Fruit & Veg)	Arcade Reproductions
6	Arcade Furnishers Ltd	Arcade Furnishers	Arcade Furnishers	Milligans Restaurant
6A	Arcade Furnishers Ltd	Arcade Furnishers	Arcade Furnishers	J & R Car Radio
7				
8	Arcade Furnishers Ltd	Arcade Furnishers	Arcade Furnishers	Bee Video Systems (Video)
West Alley				
1	E.C.Pomfret (Shoes)	Collectors Corner	Acorn Antiques	Collectors Corner
2	C.Wray (Shoe Repairs)	Old Exchange Antiques Curios	The Old Exchange Antiques Curios	C.Wray (Shoe Repairs)
3	C.Wray (Shoe Repairs)	C.Wray (Shoe Repairs)	C.Wray (Shoe Repairs)	C.Wray (Shoe Repairs)
4	C.Wray (Shoe Repairs)	C.Wray (Shoe Repairs)	C.Wray (Shoe Repairs)	C.Wray (Shoe Repairs)
5	C.Wray (Shoe Repairs)	C.Wray (Shoe Repairs)	C.Wray (Shoe Repairs)	C.Wray (Shoe Repairs)
6	C.Wray (Shoe Repairs)	C.Wray (Shoe Repairs)	C.Wray (Shoe Repairs)	C.Wray (Shoe Repairs)
7	Charrington Fuel Office	Charrington Fuel Office	Charrington Fuel Office	Charrington Fuel Office (NF)
	Antique Market	Antique Market	Antique Market	Antique Market
Ref	Goad Plan Revised Oct 1973	Goad Plan Revised Sept 1977	Goad Plan Revised April 1981	Goad Plan Revised Feb 1983

SHOPS & BUSINESSES: 1987-1996

	1987	1988	1989	1996
Arcade				
1	The Book Bug	The Book Bug	The Book Bug	The Book Bug
1a				
2	Footcare	Footcare	Footcare	A Touch of Garnish (restaurant)
3	Arcade Sports	Arcade Sports	Arcade Sports	Arcade Sports
4	Arcade Sports	Arcade Sports	Arcade Sports	Arcade Sports
5	Fringe Benefits (Hair)	Fringe Benefits (Hair)	Fringe Benefits (Hair)	Fringe Benefits (Hair)
6	Colroys Fruit & Veg	Colroys Fruit & Veg	Colroys Fruit & Veg	Orchard House Fruit Shop
7	William H. Church (Seeds Pet Foods)	William H. Church (Seeds Pet Foods)	William H. Church (Seeds Pet Foods)	E.C.Pomfret (Shoes)
8	William H. Church (Seeds Pet Foods)	William H. Church (Seeds Pet Foods)	William H. Church (Seeds Pet Foods)	E.C.Pomfret (Shoes)
9	E.C.Pomfret (Shoes)	E.C.Pomfret (Shoes)	E.C.Pomfret (Shoes)	E.C.Pomfret (Shoes)
Front 33MP	E.C.Pomfret (Shoes)	E.C.Pomfret (Shoes)	E.C.Pomfret (Shoes)	House of Flowers
Arcade Walk				
1	The Jewelry Workshop	The Jewelry Workshop	The Jewelry Workshop	Jewelry Workshop
2	Vacant	Daydreams L/WR	South East Security (Locks)	Oh La Di D'Art (Gifts)
3	Merry Go Round (Toys Nursery)	Merry Go Round (Toys Nursery)	Merry Go Round (Toys Nursery)	Nips & Tucks
4	Lays Tea & Coffee	Lays Tea & Coffee	Tea & Coffee Shop	Just Lace (Linen)
5	Arcade Reproductions	Arcade Reproductions	Arcade Reproductions	Arcade Reproductions (Furniture)
6	Cortina Bridal + L.A. Jolie (Beauty)	Cortina Bridal + L.A. Jolie (Beauty)	Cortina Bridal + L.A. Jolie (Beauty)	Crafty Ideas (Crafts)
6A	L.A.Folie (Beauty)	L.A.Folie (Beauty)	L.A.Folie (Beauty)	Vacant
7	Herts Properties (Estate Agents)	Herts Properties (Estate Agents)	Herts Properties (Estate Agents)	South & East Securities
8	VIP Video	VIP Video	VIP Video	Body Magic
West Alley				
1	Acorn Antiques	Acorn Antiques	Acorn Antiques	Stepping Stones (S/H Goods)
2	Wrays Footwear Repairs & Print	Wrays Footwear Repairs & Print	The Dress Circle L/WR	Dress Circle (S/H Clothes)
3	Wrays Footwear Repairs & Print	Wrays Footwear Repairs & Print	Just Sew (Haberdashers)	West Alley Shoe Repair
4	Wrays Footwear Repairs & Print	Wrays Footwear Repairs & Print	C. Wray Shoe Repairs	Willow Room Gifts
5	Wrays Footwear Repairs & Print	Wrays Footwear Repairs & Print	C. Wray Shoe Repairs	Willow Room Gifts
6	Wrays Footwear Repairs & Print	Wrays Footwear Repairs & Print	Hitchin Tile & Pine Home Improvements	Vacant
7	Charrington Fuel Office (NF)	Charrington Fuel Office (NF)	Charrington Fuel Office	The Paint Shop (Art)
	Antique Market	Antique Market	Antique Market	Market Stalls
Ref	Goad Plan Revised July 1987	Goad Plan Revised August 1988	Goad Plan Revised Aug 1989	Goad Plan 1996 & Memories B.Worbey

SHOPS & BUSINESSES: 1997-2000

	1997	1998	1999	2000
Arcade				
1	The Book Bug	The Book Bug	The Book Bug	The Book Bug
1a				
2	A Touch of Garnish (restaurant)	A Touch of Garnish (restaurant)	A Touch of Garnish (restaurant)	A Touch of Garnish (restaurant)
3	Arcade Sports	Arcade Sports	Arcade Sports	Touch of Glass (Mirrors)
4	Arcade Sports	Arcade Sports	Arcade Sports	Touch of Glass (Mirrors)
5	Fringe Benefits (Hair)	Fringe Benefits (Hair)	Fringe Benefits (Hair)	Fringe Benefits (Hair)
6	Woodland Interiors (Fit Furniture)	Woodland Interiors (Fit Furniture)	Woodland Interiors (Fit Furniture)	Woodland Interiors (Fit Furniture)
7	E.C.Pomfret (Shoes)	E.C.Pomfret (Shoes)	E.C.Pomfret (Shoes)	E.C.Pomfret (Shoes)
8	E.C.Pomfret (Shoes)	E.C.Pomfret (Shoes)	E.C.Pomfret (Shoes)	E.C.Pomfret (Shoes)
9	E.C.Pomfret (Shoes)	E.C.Pomfret (Shoes)	E.C.Pomfret (Shoes)	E.C.Pomfret (Shoes)
Front 33MP	House of Flowers	House of Flowers	House of Flowers	House of Flowers
Arcade Walk				
1	Vain Glory (Jeweller)	Vain Glory (Jeweller)	Vain Glory (Jeweller)	Vain Glory (Jeweller)
2	Oh La Di D'Art (Gifts)	Oh La Di D'Art (Gifts)	Oh La Di D'Art (Gifts)	Oh La Di D'Art (Gifts)
3	Nips & Tucks	Nips & Tucks	Nips & Tucks	Nips & Tucks (Clothes & Toys)
4	Just Lace (Linen)	Just Lace (Linen)	Vacant	Vacant
5	Arcade Reproductions	Arcade Reproductions	Venus (Lingerie)	Venus (Lingerie)
6	Stamps N. Stencils (Crafts)	Stamps N. Stencils (Crafts)	Stamps, Stencils & Crafts	Stamps, Stencils & Crafts
6A	Hatters Tea Rooms	Hatters	Hatters of Hitchin (Tea Room)	Hatters of Hitchin (Tea Room)
7	Nelsons Gifts	Nelsons Gifts	Nelsons Gifts	Salvation Army
8	Body Magic	Body Magic	Body Magic Health Salon	Body Magic Health Salon
West Alley				
1	Stepping Stones (S/H Goods)	Webster Craft (Haberdashers)	Webster Craft (Haberdashers)	Webster Craft (Haberdashers)
2	Dress Circle (S/H Clothes)	Dress Circle S/H Clothing	Dress Circle S/H Clothing	Redesign S/H Clothing
3	West Alley Shoe Repair	West Alley Shoe Repair	West Alley Shoe Repair	West Alley Shoe Repair
4	Willow Room Gifts	Willow Room Gifts	Willow Room Gifts	Willow Room Gifts
5	Willow Room Gifts	Willow Room Gifts	Willow Room Gifts	Willow Room Gifts
6	Paint Shop (Paint)	Paint Shop (Paint)	Paint Shop (Wallpaper Paint)	Paint Shop (Wallpaper Paint)
7	Paint Shop (Paint)	Paint Shop (Paint)	Paint Shop (Wallpaper Paint)	Paint Shop (Wallpaper Paint)
	Disabled Car Parking	Disabled Car Parking	Disabled Car Parking	Disabled Car Parking
Ref	Goad Plan Revised Aug 1997	Goad Plan Revised Aug 1998	Goad Plan Surveyed Sept 1999	Goad Plan Revised Oct. 2000

SHOPS & BUSINESSES: 2001-2007

	2001	2007
Arcade		
1	The Book Bug (Secondhand Books)	The Book Bug (Secondhand Books)
1a		
2	A Touch of Garnish (restaurant)	A Touch of Garnish (Sandwich Bar)
3	Planet Clothing	Planet Clothing
4	Planet Clothing	Planet Clothing
5	Jolie (Hairdressers)	Fringe Benefits & La Jolie (Hairdressers)
6	Woodland Interiors (Fit Furniture)	Woodland Interiors (Furniture)
7	E.C.Pomfret & Son (Footwear)	Planet Clothing
8	E.C.Pomfret & Son (Footwear)	Planet Clothing
9	E.C.Pomfret & Son (Footwear)	Vacant
Front 33MP	House of Flowers (Florist)	O2 Mobile Phone Store
Arcade Walk		
1	Vain Glory (Jeweller)	Vain Glory (Gold & Silver Jewellery)
2	Oh La Di D'Art (Gifts)	The Ginger Jar (Wine & Tapas Bar)
3	Nips & Tucks	Nips & Tucks (Children's toys & clothing)
4	Venus (Lingerie)	Venus (Lingerie & Swimwear)
5	Venus (Lingerie)	Venus (Lingerie & Swimwear)
6	Collusions on Hair	Collusion (Men's Barber)
6A	Hatters of Hitchin (Tea Room)	Hatters (Bistro & Cafe)
7	Salvation Army (Charity Shop)	Salvation Army (Charity Shop)
8	Body Magic Health Salon	Body Magic Health Salon (Beauty Treatment)
West Alley		
1	Kratty Corner (Haberdashers)	Kratty Corner (Haberdashers)
2	Redesign S/H Clothing	Espadrille French Living
3	The Carving Studio Furniture	Classic Moment (Jewellry)
4	The Willow Room (Gifts)	The Willow Room (Gifts)
5	The Willow Room (Gifts)	The Willow Room (Gifts)
6	Planet Fitted Furniture	The Willow Room (Gifts)
7	Planet Fitted Furniture	The Willow Room (Gifts)
8		Dyspraxia Foundation
	Disabled Car Parking	Disabled Car Parking
Ref	Goad Plan Revised Oct. 2001	Survey August 2007 - Chris Parker

Sources

PRINTED SOURCES

ANON.	Calendar of Assize Records, Herts. Indictments, James I	H.M.S.O. 1975
BOYER, P.	An assessment of an archaeological excavation on land off Paynes Park, Hitchin, Hertfordshire	Brockley: Pre-Construct Archaeology 2005
BROWN, J. E.	Chantry Certificates for Hertfordshire: a transcript of The Return made by The Commissioners in the reign of Edward VI with an introduction by BROWN, J E, Vicar of Studham	
BRYANT, S. & SEDDON, V.	Hertford: Extensive Urban Assessment Report	Hertford: Hertfordshire County Council 1999
BURLEIGH, G. R. & STEVENSON, M. D.	Land to the rear of Paynes Park, Market Place and High Street, Hitchin, Hertfordshire: an archaeological desktop assessment.	Unpublished assessment report. Letchworth: North Hertfordshire District Council Museums (Report 22) 1994
CROSBY, Tony et al	Jeeves Yard: A dynasty of Hitchin Builders and Brickmakers	Streets Publishers, Baldock 2003
DAVIS, S.	Late and post-Roman burial to 19th-century brickmaking: excavations at the site of 40 Queen Street, Hitchin, SG4	Herts Archaeol/14 (2004-5)
DOUGLAS, Priscilla & HUMPHRIES, Pauline (Ed)	Discovering Hitchin	Egon Publishers Ltd 1995
EKWALL, E.	English river names	Oxford: Clarendon Press 1928
FIELD, Richard	Hitchin: A Pictorial History	Phillimore Chichester 1991
FITZPATRICK, Sue & WEST, Barry	The Street Names of Hitchin & Their Origins - Book 1	Egon Publishers Ltd 1997
FOSTER, A. M.	Herts Past and Present (3), A Brief History of Banking in Hitchin	Hertfordshire Local History Council 1962/3
FOSTER, Anthony M.	The Book of Hitchin	Barracuda Books 1981
FOSTER, Anthony M.	A Brief History of Hitchin Markets & Fairs	Hitchin Historical Society in association with NHDC Museums Service 1978
FOSTER, Anthony M. (Ed.) JOHNSON, W.B MUNBY, L.	Market Town: Hitchin in the Hertfordshire Inns Parts1, 2 Nineteenth Century	Hitchin Historical Society 1987 Hertfordshire Countryside 1962/1963
FRIEL, I.	Herts Past (13). The Hicce: an Anglo-Saxon tribe in the Hitchin area	Hertfordshire Local History Council 1982
GADD, Pat	Hitchin Past & Present	Howell's Bookshop 1978
GADD, Pat	50 Years of Change in Hitchin circa 1930 - 80	AuthorGraphics Ltd 1980
GADD, Pat	Old Hitchin Life, Vol 1 No4	Hitchin Historical Society 1986

GADD, Pat	Manuscript on Hitchin Inns	Unpublished
GADD, Pat & PIGRAM, Ron	Hitchin Inns & Incidents	P Gadd 1978
GOVER, JEB, MAWER, A. & STENTON, F. M.	The Place-names of Hertfordshire	Cambridge University Press 1938
HARTLEY, D. & ELLIOTT, M.	Life and Works of the People of England	Batsford 1904
HAYMAN, Richard	The History and Archaeology of the Iron Industry	Tempus Publishing 2005
HINE, Reginald L.	The History of Hitchin Vols 1 & 2	George Allen & Unwin Ltd 1927, 1929
HITCHIN HISTORICAL SOCIETY	The Street names of Hitchin and their origins. Book 3	Egon Publishers Ltd 1999
HOWLETT, B.	Hitchin Priory Park: the history of a landscape park and gardens.	Hitchin Historical Society 2004
LUCAS, W.	A Quaker Journal (Editors GE Bryant & GP Baker)	Hutchinson and Co Ltd. 1933
MOGG, E.	Paterson's Roads (18th Edition)	Longman 1840
MORLET, M.	Hitchin Town Centre, Hitchin Hertfordshire: geoarchaeological report	Museum of London Archaeological Service a 2003
O'CLEE, Fred	The Hitchin Household Almanac	Paternoster & Hales, 1899
OFFER, C.	King Offa in Hitchin	Hitchin: Privately printed 1992
OFFER, C.	In search of Clofesho: the case for Hitchin	Norwich: Tessa 2002
POOLE, Helen & FLECK, Alan	Old Hitchin	Eric T Moore/North Herts Museum 1976
ROBINSON, Susan	The Gatward Story	Unpublished
	Shorter Oxford English Dictionary	Oxford University Press
TOMKINS, M.	So That was Hertfordshire; Travellers' Jottings 1322-1887	Hertfordshire Publications 1998
THOMPSON, I.	Hitchin: Extensive Urban Survey revised Assessment Report	Hertford: Hertfordshire County Council 2005
WALKER, Simon	Images of England, Hitchin	Tempus Publishing Ltd. 2003
WILLIAMS, G. A. (Compiler)	Travellers in Hertfordshire	Hertfordshire County Council 1983
WILLIAMSON, T.	The Origins of Hertfordshire	Manchester University Press 2000

HITCHIN MUSEUM

Lawson Thompson Scrapbooks, Vols 1A, 1B, 3A
Loftus Barham Scrapbooks, Vols 1, 4, 5, 7
History, Topography & Directory of Buckinghamshire,
    Cambridgeshire & Hertfordshire 1864
Craven & Co Commercial Directory
Pigotts Directories
Cassey and Co Directories
Kelly's Directories
Post Office Directory
Handbook to Hitchin and the Neighbourhood   Paternoster & Hales (Various)
Hitchin Official Guides   Various
Hertfordshire Express and Bedfordshire Express,
    Newspaper Archives

Photographs, maps, plans and other ephemera

Sources

HERTFORDSHIRE ARCHIVES AND LOCAL STUDIES (HALS)

Hertfordshire Mercury Newspaper Archive
Hitchin Official Guide   1931
Hitchin Urban District Council Rate Books 1929—1961

NATIONAL ARCHIVES, KEW

Company Records

HITCHIN LIBRARY

Census Materials 1841 - 1881
Hitchin Directory
Hitchin Directory
The Official Programme of the Hitchin Celebration
    of the Coronation of the King
Handbook to Hitchin and the Neighbourhood

Paternoster & Hales 1929
Letchworth Printers 1952-3, 1960
Paternoster & Hales 1902

Paternoster & Hales 1899

CD ROM

FLECK, Alan   Exploring Hitchin   Hitchin Historical Society 2006

WIKIPEDIA

WIKIPEDIA   History of Ferrous Metallurgy. Pig Iron,   Accessed May-July 2007
(www.wikipedia.com)   Cast Iron, Wrought Iron, Blast Furnace,
                        Sand Casting, Whitesmith

GATWARD & SON HITCHIN

ABOUT THE HITCHIN HISTORICAL SOCIETY

Hitchin Historical Society, founded in 1977, currently has over 300 members. Besides
arranging meetings and visits relating to Hitchin, Hertfordshire and local history in general, it
encourages its members to undertake individual and group research on the history of their
fascinating and historic market town. **www.hitchinhistoricals.org.uk**

Index

Bold page numbers denote illustrations.

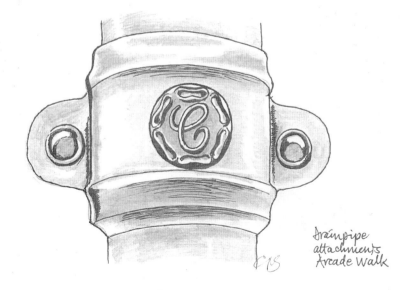

drainpipe
attachments
Arcade Walk